LEAN
INCEPTION

Editora Caroli
caroli.org

PAULO CAROLI

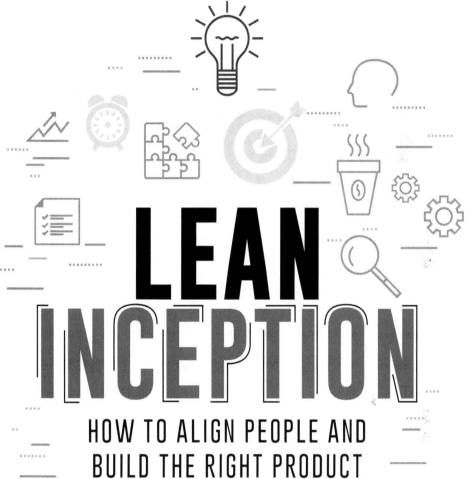

LEAN INCEPTION

HOW TO ALIGN PEOPLE AND BUILD THE RIGHT PRODUCT

Editora
Caroli
caroli.org

Copidesque
Juliana Cury Rodrigues

Proofreading
Alyne Azuma and Laura Folgueira

Graphic design, layout and cover
Vanessa Lima

Copyright © 2019 by Paulo Caroli
All the rights reserved to Editora Caroli.
Avenida Itajaí, 310 – Petrópolis
Porto Alegre, RS 90470-140, Brasil
www.caroli.org/editora
contato@caroli.org

Dados Internacionais de Catálogo na Publicação (CIP)
Angélica Ilacqua CRB-8/7057

Caroli, Paulo
    Lean Inception: how to align people and build the right product / Paulo
Caroli. – São Paulo: Editora Caroli, 2019.
    168 p. : il.

Includes bibliographical references
ISBN 978-85-94377-13-5

1. Product design 2. Product planning 3. Production planning 4. Strategic planning
I. Title

19-1780   CDD 658.575

                Index for Systematic Catalog:
              1. Product development: planning

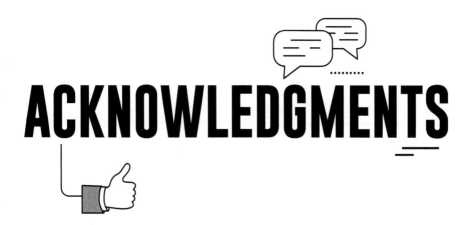

ACKNOWLEDGMENTS

THANK YOU ThoughtWorks and ThoughtWorkers for inspiring me and using my Lean Inception activities. I truly believe this amazing content emerged from a very specific context which you are part of. My special thanks to ThoughtWorks Brazil, my home country and the cradle of this work.

Thank you to those who shared their knowledge about inception workshops and made this work possible. My special thanks to Jeff Patton and Jonathan Rasmusson, whom I have the pleasure and privilege to learn from.

Thanks to everyone who read, used and shared feedback on the Lean Inception. This content evolved due to the great feedback and the shared experiences. I only realized this was something special once I heard about its success when applied by other facilitators.

Thanks to Martin Fowler for coaching me and asking for this content in English. I really appreciate your support and incentive when sharing important practices with our greater community, such as the Lean Inception.

Thanks to Patrick Sarnacke for the detailed review on this book's contents. I have really appreciated your inputs since 2008, the year you started revising some of my English writings.

Thanks to my family for the love and support while I stay in my study reading and writing, in the pursuit of learning and sharing. My special thanks to João Caroli. I can still remember my first trip after you were born. I've always loved facilitating inceptions, but I love you more and could not stay away for more than a few days. I had to make them lean in order to come home faster. You definitely inspired me!

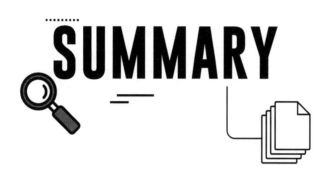

SUMMARY

FOREWORD

The naive view of agile software development is that everyone just dives in and starts writing code without spending any time at the beginning figuring out what to do.

That view, although as erroneous as it is simplistic, is based on a genuine shift in thinking. Prior to Agile's rise, serious software people advised long periods gathering the of requirements and architecture—and that happened at a time when a five-year project might wait a year or two before any code was written, let alone being released into production. The agile world has discarded such long periods of up-front analysis, but we still recognize that there is value in setting out with an initial sense of direction. The challenge is figuring out how we can do this quickly and efficiently, while remembering that nothing teaches us what we want more than an incomplete product that has been released and is in use. So, we need to balance setting direction with the knowledge that such up-front thinking is our most tentative.

At ThoughtWorks, our response has been a process called an inception. We have put together a good sample of the people who will be affected by the product and have an intensive session to set an initial direction, using a series of exercises focusing on collaboration and the capture of broad goals. Our aim is not a detailed specification, as that is exactly the kind of thing that becomes out of date as soon as code hits production. But we do want to understand what kind of outcomes we are hoping for, the features we believe drive these outcomes, and how to assess the effectiveness of our product.

With **Lean Inception**, Paulo has gathered his experience in running these inceptions over the last decade. In particular, it's focused on his work to boil the inception down to its essence, concentrating the activity on a single, if very intensive, week of work. Paulo shares how he makes this work, through writing a product vision, capturing personas, understanding the user's journeys, and developing high-level features. The result isn't a detailed plan of work, which we quickly find falls into irrelevance. It is a guiding set of goals to set us off in the right direction. It doesn't plan out a final product, with all the features that our users will need, instead it focuses on an initial product that we can release and learn from—the Minimum Viable Product. This product acts as the starting point for evolving a richer and more capable version, and again we can use lean inceptions to help with each step of this evolution.

In this book, you'll find Paulo's experience harvested from six years of running these lean inceptions. There is a timetable for a typical week of activities, details of the exercises to do, and tips to help the team learn from the release of the Minimum Viable Product. The efforts of the week are summarized in an MVP Canvas which acts as simple output and summary of the work. Armed with Paulo's experience, you can practice this technique and adapt it to suit your circumstances.

MARTIN FOWLER

Chief Scientist of ThoughtWorks.

martinfowler.com

THE AGILE WORLD HAS
DISCARDED SUCH LONG
PERIODS OF UP-FRONT
ANALYSIS, BUT WE STILL
RECOGNIZE THAT THERE IS
VALUE IN SETTING
OUT WITH AN INITIAL
SENSE OF DIRECTION.

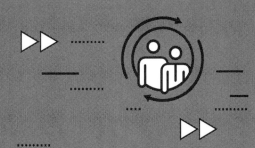

INTRODUCTION

WHAT YOU WILL FIND HERE

Reading this book is very easy: from the beginning to the end! This is a short and practical book. As the title says: *Lean*.

The book is structured in three main parts: "Building the Right Product," "Preparing for the Workshop," and "Running the Lean Inception"—followed by the appendices.

On the first part—"Building the Right Product"—I tell my story with inceptions and why I created the Lean Inception concept. The book is based on the concept of MVP, short for Minimum Viable Product. The chapter named after it presents the concept and tells its story, as well as my view on MVP and the evolution of lean products.

The second part—"Preparing for the Workshop"—explains in detail the collaborative workshop format that will help you understand, align and plan the building of the lean product. Maybe it's the beginning of an agile project in a big corporation, or the alignment on what to build in a small start-up. The collaborative and dynamic style of Lean Inception is the chef's secret to this recipe.

And, in the final part—"Running the Lean Inception"—there is the recipe! Lean Inception is a sequence of collaborative and dynamic activities that will build the MVP canvas, a visual representation of the lean product's evolution and creation plan. Every step of this recipe is detailed matching the order of chapters, starting with "Write the Product Vision," and ending with "Build the MVP Canvas."

The appendices can be read before, during or after you read the entire book. A book named *Lean* forces the author to write an appendix. I consider the whole content of this book essential. However, in the appendix you can find what was added with time, based on the readers' feedback.

The first one brings you a real example of understanding and planning a lean product from the Lean Inception recipe, done in a super-lean inception: in only six hours! Some readers have told me that first they read this appendix and then they read the book from the start. Lastly, there is the glossary of the terms mentioned in the book and some icebreaker activities.

HOW DID THIS BOOK COME UP?

"The road map for innovation in the twenty-first century. The ideas in *The Lean Startup* will help create the next industrial revolution," said Steve Blank[1] about *The Lean Startup* book, by Eric Ries.

I fully agree with Blank and dare to add: product development based on the MVP concept is the pillar for this new revolution.

In *The Lean Startup*, Ries presents MVP as a key piece of the build-measure-learn cycle, as illustrated below, where MVP is represented as the artifact being built.

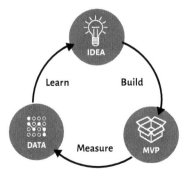

---

1   Steve Blank is an entrepreneur and academic researcher of entrepreneurship on Silicon Valley, California, USA. Available in: <https://pt.wikipedia.org/wiki/Steve_Blank>. Access in: July, 2019.

After being **built**, the MVP is put to test with its users. With this, we will have data that will make it possible to **measure** its usage and, therefore, generate the desired **learning**.

On *Lean UX* (2013), Jeff Gothelf and Josh Seiden share a very efficient model to describe what we are trying to **measure** and **learn** from the MVP (to validate a hypothesis). For example, I have been using the following adapted template for some time:

We believe this MVP will get_____
(expected result).
_____
We will know that this has happened based on _____
(metrics to validate the business hypotheses).
_____

In the Lean Startup movement, I found good answers about **learning** and **measuring**, but I lacked something to direct me to "what to **build**." That's how Lean Inception came about.

By experimenting with different inception activities and seeking support in Design Thinking, I have created a sequence of activities to help a team define the features of MVP.

Then I shared this sequence of activities—as a recipe to be followed—with some colleagues and received confirmation that the recipe helped them as well. I asked for feedback, sought improvements, made changes, and even made some adjustments to the nomenclature.

After sharing with hundreds of people and working with the feedback received, the Lean Inception workshop emerged—a sequence of activities for the creation of lean products heavily influenced by Design Thinking and Lean Startup.

There were many blog posts (starting in 2010), a workshop, an e-book and the first edition of a printed book in Portuguese—*Direto ao Ponto: Criando produtos de forma enxuta*— was released in 2014. One year later, reviews, improvements and the second edition of book in Portuguese came about. From 2015 on I started to share more about Lean Inception in English and Spanish (through blog posts and e-books). And in 2016, I started writing the article "Lean Inception" on Martin Fowler's website[2].

At that time, ThoughtWorks had over 5,000 consultants in 41 offices in 14 countries. From the feedback of Martin Fowler himself and several colleagues at ThoughtWorks and other organizations—among which were Jonathan Rasmussan and Jeff Patton, major influencers on my work with inceptions—I improved the structure and vocabulary of the article and the Lean Inception workshop. This led me to publish the book *Lean Inception* in English, with a new structure and more content.

Then, in late 2018, with even more feedback from the many Lean Inception facilitators in Brazil (the country I was living in and where I was applyig the book content on a daily basis), I released the *Lean Inception* book in Portuguese. It was a major success: #1 in Amazon.com.br[3] sales for many months since its release.

In 2019 I moved from Brazil to Spain and updated *Lean Inception* to this new version you have in your hands. I'll share more about Lean Inception in English and Spanish—the Brazilian market already knows and use it—a lot.

What else?

---

2 Available in: <https://martinfowler.com/articles/lean-inception/>. Access in: Jul. 2019.

3 Available in: <https://www.caroli.org/lean-inception-o-mais-vendido-em-empreendedorismo-na-amazon/>. Access in: Jul. 2019.

I continue to be very involved with Lean Inceptions. As I focus on MVP, I ended up touching on some related topics: digital transformation, innovation, entrepreneurship, strategy, continuous delivery, DevOps, among many others.

There is a lot of content linked to that, but I want to keep this book lean. For this reason, I do not intend to add more to it, but I'll share related content on my site. Check it out the news on **www.caroli.org**.

Have a good reading and welcome to the Lean Inception facilitators' group!

BUILDING THE
RIGHT PRODUCT

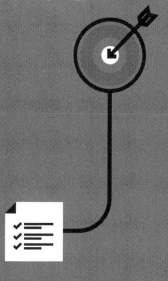

CREATING PRODUCTS THAT MATTER

Agile projects emphasize the early and continuous delivery of a valuable product, whose value comes from business objectives and the needs of customers. Lean Startup product creation aids this by promoting the incremental release of an MVP (Minimum Viable Product)—a simple version of a product that is given to users in order to validate the key business assumptions.

But how do we work out what should be in MVP and kick start an agile project as quickly as possible? How do we ensure the team will start creating the product with a shared understanding and an effective plan?

I designed **Lean Inception** to answer these questions.

INCEPTION, THE BEGINNING
OF AN AGILE PROJECT

There is no up-front work in the naive agile, but in practice we realize there has to be some. For ThoughtWorks[4], Inception is that "some." Since I joined ThoughtWorks in 2006, I realized that all agile projects in the company started in a similar way. The project team would get together for a few weeks, going through many activities prior to starting the delivery work: this was the inception.

4 A global information technology consultancy focused on agile software development.

The ThoughtWorks inception was primarily developed by Luke Barrett around 2004. Both Jonathan Rasmusson (author of *The Agile Samurai*) and Jeff Patton (author of *User Story Mapping*) worked at ThoughtWorks for a while, and they described and further developed inception techniques in their books, from which I learned a lot.

Our inceptions vary from project to project, but they usually generate alignment between the business and the technical people, as well as creating an ordered list of user stories with estimates together with a release plan. And I was very satisfied to facilitate these agile inceptions this way until 2011, the year my son was born. The thing is, I was the inception facilitator, but the inception would take from two to four weeks. And I could not stay away from home for more than a week. I had to make the inceptions leaner somehow make them fit in one week.

I was going on my first trip after my son was born. On a long flight from São Paulo to San Francisco, I read *The Lean StartUp*, by Eric Ries. In it I found the perfect excuse to reduce the inception length and return home after one week.

WHY IS IT CALLED THE LEAN INCEPTION?

This new inception style is definitely a shift from the 2006 version. The team neither writes nor estimates user stories anymore. While experimenting with this new style, the name "inception" gave everyone the wrong message. I needed a different name.

The new inception style is **lean** for two reasons:

1. The duration is shorter, removing everything that was not about the product (such as architecture, project etc.), making it lean.

2. The end result of the inception is the understanding of the MVP, a main concept from the Lean Startup movement.

Therefore, the new inception style had a clear leading name: Lean Inception.

WHY A LEAN INCEPTION?

A lean inception is useful when the team needs to iteratively develop an MVP. Although the term is often misunderstood, the main characteristic of an MVP is being something we build in order to learn whether it is worthwhile to continue building a product. So we choose features based on our assumptions of what is valuable to our users. For this we need to understand who our users are, what activities performed by them are supported by the product and how to measure if they find the product useful.

After facilitating more than 300 Lean Inceptions and follow up projects and initiatives before and after the workshop, we have found out that it is very valuable in two main circumstances:

1. Large projects consider a lean inception valuable to start quickly and be oriented to work in a lean style. Such a start helps to discover and test what features are truly valued by their users.

2. Smaller organizations (such as startups) use lean inceptions to take an idea that has been tested by some pre-software MVPs and develop it into a software product.

This workshop is specifically about understanding an MVP, it doesn't replace ideation sessions, customer research, architectural review, or competitive analysis. It is one specific technique that is part of understanding what it takes to build a successful product. Exactly how it fits in with these other activities depends very much on the specific context of your organization and the particular development effort you are working on.

THE LEAN INCEPTION AGENDA

The lean inception consists of a series of activities, typically scheduled over the course of a week. I'll explain each activity in the "Running the Lean Inception" section.

LEAN INCEPTION - TIMETABLE EXAMPLE

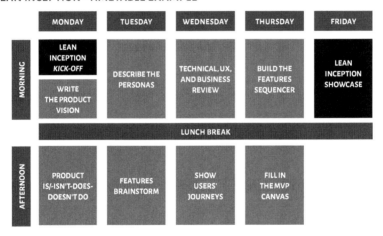

This is an example of a timetable, please do not treat it as a fixed thing, but let it serve as a good example of how things might flow.

MINIMUM VIABLE PRODUCT

A new way to create and develop products, delivering only the minimum viable, has been instrumental in helping thousands of entrepreneurs launch fantastic products. Check out successful examples like iPhone, Facebook, Spotify, Ainbnb, EasyTaxi, Zappos, among many others. Their creators have worked this way since the beginning of time, when these products were not yet (extremely) famous.

The benefits of delivering the minimum viable will help you get your product to the market much faster, minimizing costs and developing the product based on your users' feedback.

The great idea of creating only the minimum viable of a product has a name and nickname: minimum viable product (full name) and MVP (nickname).

MVP is the simplest version of a product that can be made available to validate a small set of assumptions on the business. Basically, you don't want to waste time, money or effort building a product that won't meet your expectations. For that reason, you need to understand and validate your hypothesis about the business. MVP helps you do it and learn the fastest way.

Different from products created using traditional methods, usually taking too much time and effort for prototyping, analysis, and elaboration, the goal of MVP is only to validate the first step—the minimum product—which is far less developed than the final version. MVP focuses on the minimum but viable product to verify if the direction is correct. The initial set of functionality needed for hypothesis validation and for learning more about the business.

THE ORIGIN

The idea of MVP is originally connected to the ideas that became popular with the Toyota's lean manufacture style. Steve Blank, an entrepreneur from Silicon Valley, created a methodology based on client development. That was the beginning of the Lean Startup movement, which hit its apex with Eric Ries and his book named after the movement.

While Eric Ries turned MVP popular since the publication of *Lean StartUp*, the expression had been in use for many years before the movement came to life, especially amongst startups with their entrepreneurs and stakeholders from Silicon Valley. The expression **minimum viable product** came up for the first time in 2000 in Willian Junk's article, "The Dynamic Balance Between Cost, Schedule, Features, and Quality in Software Development Projects, Computer Science."

MVP INCREMENTS

MVP does not mean that the product won't evolve and enhance its features. On the contrary, the idea behind MVP is product enhancement guided by proven hypothesis validation.

Course correction or confirmation is what is going to guide the following enhancements. These enhancements are MVP: new minimum products added to the minimum products already validated.

Once more, minimum products, but viable to make decisions about the product evolution. The product now is extended, maybe with a bigger user database, allowing the validation of hypothesis to be even more elaborated.

It is very important to understand that the MVP promotes an evolutionary creation. Ergo, the architecture as well as the building tools of the product must allow this continuous and progressive evolution.

In 2010, Jez Humble and David Farley published *Continuous Delivery*. In this book the authors discuss a fast and frequent delivery process, allowing the incremental creation of software products. They define "continuous delivery" as a discipline of software development that promotes quicker and more frequent deliveries.

In spite of the fact that *Continuous Delivery* details software products and the workflow for their creation, the essential idea of continuous delivery is the same that Eric Ries recommends on *The Lean Startup*: fast cycles to validate hypothesis.

THINK BIG,
START SMALL,
LEARN FAST!

Fast and frequent cycles, allowing very short release periods and low costs of experimentation. But it is not easy to implement this kind of approach. And the creators of MVP are going to need structures and practices different from those used traditionally in products with a slow release cycle.

This book focuses on analysis and effective planning activities based on MVP. *Continuous Delivery* is the bible if you want to understand the necessary tools for software product creation and evolution. But even more, the techniques and the learnings shared by the authors of *Continuous Delivery* are being applied for other kinds of products, not only software. The same goes for this book.

SMALL HYPOTHESIS, GREAT BUSINESSES

The product is built incrementally, with recently-created MVPs being added to the existing product. With MVP enhancements, the continuous and incremental delivery provides an increase of value of the product over time, while the creation process for traditional products does not provide any value up to the end, when the product is ready in its whole.

This image shows how MVP offers small validations in the long run, while the more traditional style of product creation only offers validation of the whole in the end. But please do not get caught in this example, because real products are not as simple as one step to another relatively similar one.

We can imagine another situation: the MVP for crossing a river. A simple solution to crossing a small stream is to lay a wooden beam across it. And it makes a great MVP. Besides allowing a small stream or a river to be crossed, it is a simple way to validate the location for building the bridge. Perhaps lay more than one wooden beam on different locations and validate which one will have more usage.

MVP promotes an incremental approach in which only a small part of the general hypothesis is tested at the same time. Each one of these hypotheses is designed, created, and prepared to be added to the product, in order to generate useful data to its own decision-making, learning and validation.

In essence, an idea (or great business hypothesis) is sequenced in a series of small, simpler, and, hence, easier to understand hypotheses. The outcome is: the simpler hypotheses are more quickly elaborated, and become readily available in the product for the final user. For instance: if there was a bridge in this place, how many pedestrians would use it in a week?

In this case, the final user (or who validates the MVP) provides data for validating the enhancement of the product. This validation is essential for two reasons: 1- corrections and changes can be made in an initial stage of the product, instead of only appearing in the end of conception, reducing the product's risk; 2- the complexity of the analysis for the hypotheses is reduced.

The product's creators and final users have early access to something functional and viable. Thus, the decision of the next steps and increments of the product are based on the product itself, instead of being hypotheses about other hypotheses. And this work pattern in small enhancements of the products and its hypothesis allows building much more elaborated products, with small but very well-founded steps.

A SAMPLE MVP EVOLUTION PLAN

The product is built incrementally, with newly-created MVPs being added to consolidated existing product. The last released MVP has a positive result. Then the team follows the MVP evolution plan, creating the next set of features for the next MVP release.

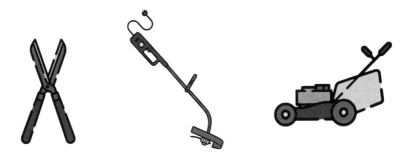

This figure shows how MVP offers small validations over time, while more traditional product creation only validates the final product. Traditional product would focus on the final version, for example, the nice lawn rover represents the final product.

The shears are the first MVP. Is there any grass to cut? Is there anyone to handle a simple grass cutting apparatus? The validation of these hypotheses drives the evolution of the product to the next MVP. Perhaps, something more convenient: a grass-cutting apparatus with a cable. How about adding wheels to it? And so on, evolving the product from MVP to MVP.

The most important and valuable feedback is a negative answer. Is there any grass to cut? No. In such case, the shears will not be used. By the way, a nice and expensive lawn rover wouldn't be used as well. Your hypothesis is false, so a fully evolved product would have been a big waste of time and money!

This example illustrates how MVP promotes an incremental approach in which only a small part of a more comprehensive idea is tested at the same time. Each of these MVPs are designed, created and prepared to be available for some users, adding more (validated) functionality to it. In essence, the idea of a product is sequenced in a series of smaller validations, and, therefore, it is easier to understand, create, and account for. And it is worth remembering that fortunately software is not manufacturing. In the software world, a lawn rover can be created by adding wheels, engine and a cable to simple shears.

THINK BIG, START SMALL

It is important to have a broader view of the product: complete, comprehensive, with many features for many types of users, meeting many business objectives.

Think big, start small, learn fast!

It is extremely important to have a broad view, to think big. However, you should start small. Take a short step and learn from it. This step is the MVP.

MVP exists to validate hypotheses, so that you gather real usage data and learn fast. In this context, less is more. Do not waste time, money or effort creating the wrong product!

The product can meet more than one business objective, work for different personas, have many functionalities. But an MVP must validate a hypothesis, prove one idea, and verify that it meets what is expected.

M is minimal, so most likely there is only one hypothesis, only a small aspect of the business, for a specific segment of users with only one or few features.

See in the following image the representation of a product elaborated via MVP. Each small box is a validated MVP via usage feedback, business interest and technical possibilities.

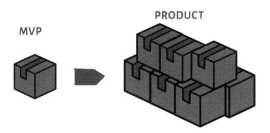

The product will grow and have more functionality (represented in the image as the stacked boxes). This happens from MVP to MVP. Or rather, from validated MVP to validated MVP. That is, each increment of the product must be validated. Do not add something that was not validated to the product!

VALUABLE, USABLE AND FEASIBLE

The MVP is at the intersection between valuable, usable, and feasible, representing, respectively, business interest, acceptance (and admiration) of product users, and what can be built.

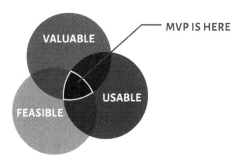

Valuable: Business people think about the commercial value of a product. Typically, these people have a vision of the business and think of MVPs as an incremental step-by-step for product creation. In this context, business people influence the MVP so that, even if it is minimal, it already achieves the return on the expected investment (or at least it demonstrates that it is in the desired direction for the business).

Usable: Any and all functionality must be tailored according to the needs, desires, and limitations of users. Something usable is based on an explicit understanding of people, their tasks and the environments of which they are part.

Feasible: The solution proposed to meet the business and the users only makes sense if it is feasible, if there are technology and knowledge to elaborate it. It does not make sense to define an MVP if you do not know how it will be built.

THE "WOW" FACTOR

The "wow" factor is what makes your product stand out in the market, what wins its users and turns them into avid promoters of your brand. It is what literally makes people say "wow!"

Think of the iPhone when it was released. It had the "wow" factor. Its users would say: "Wow! Full, touch screen... Look how cool!"

Think of the first people who asked for a taxi via website. They said: "Wow, I just added my address, clicked OK, and the cab arrived."

The "wow" factor is important for the success of a product. For an MVP, it's even more important! See the example of the iPhone 1, the MVP of the iPhone. The iPhone 1 had no third-party app (the app platform was not even

THE "WOW" FACTOR
IS IMPORTANT FOR
THE SUCCESS OF
A PRODUCT. FOR AN
MVP, IT'S EVEN
MORE IMPORTANT!

ready). It had no GPS integration and the calls were worse than in competing handsets.

But the iPhone 1 had the "wow" factor. People used and offered feedback. Its users—the early adopters—were the main promoters of the product.

People queued for the release of the iPhone 2, iPhone 3, and so on. This is because of the "wow" factor, which turns users into promoters, expanding expectation and desire for the next increment.

So it should be with MVPs. Each MVP should have the following factors: feasible, valuable, usable, and "wow".

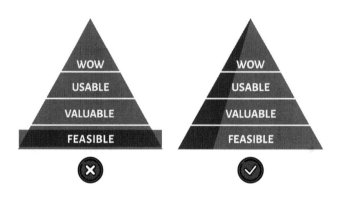

The illustration above reiterates the importance of these four factors—feasible, valuable, usable and "wow"—in each MVP.

MVP is a thin slice of the product, containing each one of these factors. Do not think of the MVP as a layer of the product (image on the left); for example, first deliver what is feasible, then elaborate another factor, then another, and finally, look for the "wow" factor.

Build the MVP as shown on the right side of the image, a small slice of the whole view, which contemplates the four factors: feasible, valuable, usable, and "wow."

> Delivering an MVP does not mean that the product is bad, simple, incompetent. Do not confuse unfinished with bad, simple with simplistic, incomplete with incompetent. The MVP should be feasible (to be created), easily usable, generate a lot of value and be awesome—"wow!"

Another example of an MVP with "wow" factor is Facebook. But you need to go back to the beginning of the website, the MVP. See in the pictures below the beginning of Facebook, or rather, the beginning of TheFacebook.com.

The beginning of Facebook illustrates the idea of a thin slice of MVP. Look how simple, unfinished, incomplete. However, it was feasible, usable, had value, and was incredible. WOW, users wanted more!

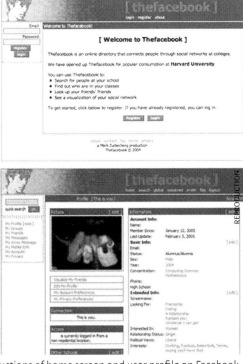

Reproductions of home screen and user profile on Facebook, in 2004.

The MVP must be feasible (to be created), easily usable, generate a lot of value and be incredible—"wow!"

BE CAREFUL NOT TO BREAK IT

Initial impressions about something are hard to undo. First impressions are very important. You want to leave a good one of your product, your MVP. You want the "wow" factor. And you absolutely want to avoid the opposite: a flaw that will leave marks.

"Fail and learn fast." Use extreme caution when using this phrase. There are ok failures and bad ones. No one wants a big mistake, one that has no fix and leaves your client with a very bad impression.

"Validate and learn fast." I prefer that phrase. In that case, you'll create an MVP that helps you validate something, but does not let the user "break" into an error in your product.

Consider again the example of the wooden bridge. The MVP managed to validate it if someone would cross the creek on a wooden beam. This MVP also helped identify the best place to put this wooden beam, this bridge. But the product has evolved. And you validated each MVP, each hypothesis: Would bikes or motorcycles also use this wooden bridge? What about four-wheeled vehicles?

And the bridge evolves from MVP to MVP... Until is collapsed! A heavy truck tried crossing the wooden bridge, and the bridge collapsed as it did not support the weight. If you had designed and built it in a traditional way, considering all the vehicles in the area, you might have built a concrete bridge and the truck would not be in that situation (stuck in a collapsed bridge).

What a difficult scenario. This argument covers the benefits of working with MVP. But note that the MVP has a V. V is for viable. The minimal viable product

LEAN INCEPTION | PAULO CAROLI

for something. A wooden bridge that does not support five tons cannot receive any vehicle heavier than five tons.

Placing a board "Maximum weight 5 tons" is not enough. A balance before the bridge can identify a truck that weighs over five tons. Maybe a balance and a gate that closes when it identifies a vehicle above the allowable weight. Two more features that, added to MVP, would avoid this error.

But the bridge would still fall if two three-ton trucks crossed at the same time. Do you realize the technical difficulty?

It is a technical difficulty, a usability challenge, and it involves the business. I will not discuss the solution to this challenge here: validate whether heavy vehicles also need and can use the bridge without collapsing it. This example is a metaphor to help you reflect about your product, your MVP.

You must think about the features that will not let your bridge fall. If it does, it was not an MVP. It was less than that, as it was not viable, and your users should not have been exposed to it. You need to validate your MVP without letting the bridge fall!

LEGACY AND ORGANIZED BLOCKS

Sometimes the new product is a new version of some legacy, something that already exists but needs improvement. Or the product evolves so quickly that its architecture, its internal structure (even if well elaborated) needs to be reorganized. Typically, products in this category are represented as logically stacked blocks and layers.

Even if the MVP is incomplete from the point of view of the final product, it must respect the blocks and layers that represent the structure of the product.

AN MVP MUST BE FEASIBLE
(TO BE CREATED), EASILY
USABLE, GENERATE
A LOT OF **VALUE**, AND BE
INCREDIBLE—"**WOW!**"

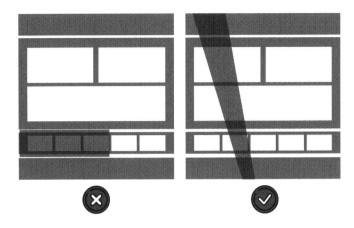

As shown in the previous image, the MVP should not be elaborated block by block to compose the overall product. Build the MVP as shown in the image on the right side of the image. You should respect the architecture, but build the end-to-end MVP with a complete experience.

That means the product is not architected block by block, but rather MVP to MVP, so that block architects (the technical people who decide the internal parts of the product) can evolve the structure of the product as needed.

SALES FUNNEL – AARRR

Sales Funnel is a representation of the flow and quantity of people in your sales process, from acquisition to referral.

AARRR (or pirate metrics) is an acronym for funnel metrics created by Dave McClure to better understand and serve the consumers of your product or service.

These five metrics—Acquisition, Activation, Retention, Revenue, and Referral, which form the acronym AARRR—represent the interactions of your customer with your product.

According to McClure, a successful startup is able to optimize each of these five metrics. He recommends collecting and analyzing these metrics separately.

» **Acquisition**: Number of people who visited your product or service.

» **Activation**: Number of people who had a good initial experience.

» **Retention**: Number of people who came back to learn more.

» **Revenue**: Number of people who engaged in revenue generating activity.

» **Referral**: Number of people recommending it to other users.

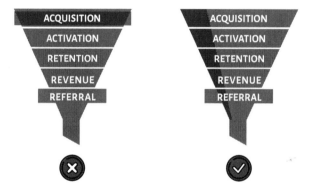

An MVP must validate all steps of the sales funnel, as illustrated on the right side of the image above.

Be careful not to insist on a business that does not convert, a false positive. False positive is something that presents a good beginning, but never becomes good business, with a lot of revenue and recommendation. This risky scenario is illustrated by the image on the left, where an MVP contemplates only one step of the sales funnel.

SCHEDULE A LEAN INCEPTION!

"For every complex problem, there is a clear, simple and wrong answer."

— H. L. Mencken

It's not easy to come up with the MVP. You should have a broad view of the product and the business; validate a hypothesis; think about the increments; consider feasible, usable, valuable, and "wow"; think about the blocks that fit; pay attention to the sales funnel etc. This book shares years of experience helping groups align MVP in a collaborative way and with their different perspectives. This is what happens in a Lean Inception.

PREPARING FOR
THE WORKSHOP

THE LEAN INCEPTION WORKSHOP

In a single week of collaborative work, the team will understand the product objectives, the main users, and the high-level functional scope such that an incremental release strategy of MVPs can be identified.

During the Inception workshop, dynamic activities take place to define goals, strategies and the scope of the product, as well as mapping and prioritizing the desirable features to be incrementally delivered, building the MVPs. The main goal of the workshop is to make the team discover and understand collectively the scope of what is going to be developed. In the end, the team should have chemistry and a clearer view of the path to follow.

The Lean Inception workshop guides the participants towards understanding and planning for the incremental delivery of MVPs. The workshop organizes ideas and features in a model that seeks to understand the main purpose of the product, considering the journeys of the users and incremental value delivery. Like a cookbook, with rapid and effective sequenced activities, the workshop will enable the team to:

» Describe the product vision
» Prioritize the business goal
» Describe the main users, their profiles and their needs
» Explore the main features

» Detail perceptions of uncertainty, effort, user value, and business value by feature

» Describe the most important user journeys

» Create an incremental product enhancement plan, driven by MVP

The following chapters explore each of these points' concept and activity.

COLLABORATION

Collaborating is the act of working together to perform a task and reach common goals. The success of an Inception is directly connected to the capacity of the group to collaborate effectively in each activity described in this book.

The Inception proposes a collaborative process of discovery and elucidation in which people involved in it work together in a sequence of activities to understand the options and elaborate MVPs. The activities presented in the following chapters represent structured collaboration methods, seeking a creative environment, while sharing knowledge, learning, and building alignment. The activities aim to build up the team success, as they get involved in detailing and resolving each step towards MVP.

HAVE FUN WITH ICEBREAKERS

Never underestimate the power of having fun. By having fun and laughing, your stress levels decrease significantly and you are much more open to working with other people. When you're happy and relaxed, you are much more open to trying new things and thereby increase your participation in this highly interactive workshop: the Lean Inception.

To the extent you want to be a part of engaging people deeply and fully with fun and effective activities, you will yourself be invited to a journey of highly participative sessions. Keeping this in mind, you need to break the ice and get the participants into the right state of mind. Icebreakers help to create a friendly environment and make people more comfortable to participate in the activities that will follow.

Icebreakers are quick and fun activities that can be run to warm up the team and promote group interaction. It is a good starter for any team meeting. It is extra valuable for early stages of team building, which is typically the case for the Lean Inception workshop.

You should select an icebreaker activity to match the needs of your Inception moment. On the first days, I recommend activities that focus on sharing information, such as names and hobbies. After lunchtime, you should select an icebreaker to wake everyone up. And finally, get to know the icebreakers with a simple message, such as "complex systems are hard to handle" or "written documentation is not enough." Besides being fun and energetic, they deliver important messages.

Below is an example of an great icebreaker for introductions. The appendix presents more icebreaker activities and ideas.

PUNCTUAL PAULO

This is a quick activity to help team members remember each other's names. This is how it works:

1. Ask the participants to think about an adjective that begins with the same letter as their name.

2. Form a circle and ask each participant to say his/her name with the adjective, in turns ("Hi, I'm Punctual Paulo!").

3. After all the participants speak, ask them to go clockwise telling the name and adjective for the person next to them.

4. After a few turns, ask the participants to repeat step 3 going counter-clockwise.

Besides sharing some laughs and breaking the ice, this activity will also help the team to associate peoples' names with an adjective, making it easier to remember them.

PLACING

Do not underestimate the value of face-to-face interaction. Innovative technologies, such as videoconferencing and online shared documents, facilitate remote work between people. However, face-to-face interaction during Inception allows hard work in activities, guaranteeing that everybody will be present and actively participating.

When everyone is in the same room, the level of participation increases. You cannot simply sit down in a corner, turn your back to the meeting, and do some other thing. Face-to-face meetings tend to be shorter and more efficient than remote meetings.

Understandings and misunderstandings are better grasped. Facial and body expressions add to the written and verbal communication. In general, face-to-face meetings help the team get to the point.

The sequence of activities to reach the MVP is long. Collaboration and results are positively surprising when everyone is physically in the same room. Do everything you can to get everyone involved in the same environment, interacting face-to-face during Inception.

THE WAR ROOM

Keep the same room allocated to the team during the intense period of Inception. This is commonly called the *war room*.

The room must accommodate the team comfortably. There must be a table and a clear wall. There must also be flipcharts, index cards and colored Post-Its, paper and pens for everyone in the room.

The war room sets the environment for collaborative activities. It also avoids any waste of time when people move from one room to another. All information is created and remains in the same place.

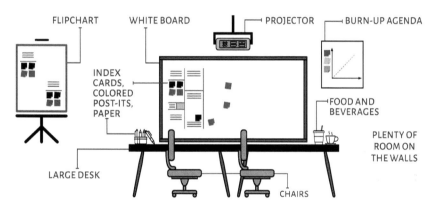

It is important to keep information in the same room, avoiding its transportation and premature documentation. Everyone can and should take hand-written notes (index cards, Post-Its, flipcharts, etc.) and put them on the wall and tables, so that the information will be visible to everybody.

COLORED POST-ITS

Make notes on colored Post-Its or index cards. Write them down and put them on the table or on the wall. Gather people around them. Talk about them. Write a little more. Group them. Separate them. Tear them down and start again.

Use different colors. Reorganize them. The collaboration born from such a simple display cannot be reached by any digital means.

There is no substitute to writing, rewriting, grouping or tearing colored Post-Its. It promotes interaction amongst people and helps the creative experimental process, in which the path is being built without the fear of trying, making mistakes or redoing things. As soon as the information goes to the computer, it does not return to the paper. That reduces the interaction among people because there is nothing on the table or on the walls, visible to everyone, and that can be easily torn down, regrouped, or rewritten.

THE INCEPTION FACILITATOR ROLE

Well-orchestrated workshops have two things in common: 1- someone thought about their structure, and 2- someone facilitates them. The remainder of this book covers a good structure for an Inception. This section unveils some thoughts about the Inception facilitator role.

The facilitator's role during the Inception workshop is focused on providing a guide "to lead the discussion" for the participants during the workshop. In order to do this, the facilitator is someone with great deal of familiarity and experience with the workshop format, its collaborative nature and the sequence of activities to be carried out.

But beware: to lead the discussion does not mean that the facilitator is the main participant, rather it means being a guide to promote the flow of ideas and activate conversations among everyone involved in the workshop.

Consequently, the work of the facilitator focuses heavily on making the Inception workshop participants take responsibility, leadership and collaboration throughout all the planned activities.

THE **INCEPTION** PROPOSES A COLLABORATIVE PROCESS OF **DISCOVERY AND ELUCIDATION** IN WHICH PEOPLE INVOLVED IN IT **WORK TOGETHER** IN A SEQUENCE OF ACTIVITIES TO UNDERSTAND THE OPTIONS AND ELABORATE MVPs.

But how should a facilitator behave? Here are some characteristics of the facilitator work during the workshop:

» The facilitator should have a higher level of vocal participation when explaining the process of Inception, introducing the activities, and also when answering questions about what is expected during the workshop and its activities.

» During the various discussions that will take place, the facilitator should take a completely neutral position, without interfering at all during the decision making process. By contrast, the approach taken by the facilitator during discussions should focus on helping the group follow the activities, identify their needs, solve their associated problems, and make decisions about it.

» To achieve this, the facilitator provides structure to the activities and interactions of the participants, so they can reach the expected results in each activity effectively.

» Throughout the Inception, the facilitator uses various techniques to give fluidity to the activities and close them, in order to reach the expected results (e.g. brainstorming[5] and pomodoro techniques[6]).

» Finally, the facilitator controls the use of everything needed in the workshop: Post-Its, flip charts, markers, and also has special ability to organize spaces, moving chairs, rearranging tables, and accommodating wall space.

---

5 *Brainstorming*. Available in: <https://en.wikipedia.org/wiki/Brainstorming>. Access in: Jul. 2019.

6 *Pomodoro Technique*. Available in: <https://en.wikipedia.org/wiki/Pomodoro_Technique>. Access in: Jul. 2019.

In other words, the goal of the facilitator is to support the participants so that they can perform exceptionally well in each activity planned for the Inception workshop, focusing on the process and content, and ensuring that the latter is generated according to the expectations and goals.

Check out a few more facilitations techniques for Lean Inception in: **www. caroli.org/en/facilitation-techniques-lean-inception**.

PARKING LOT

The Parking Lot helps to track any items, ideas and issues that are raised during an activity, but it may not be useful to discuss at that specific moment in the Inception. It is an essential toolkit for the facilitator as it provides a polite way to say "yes, I heard you. But this is not important at this moment."

The facilitator should introduce the concept of parking lot either at the beginning of the Lean Inception or whenever the first conversation goes off track. Write "Parking Lot" on a flip chart and place it on the wall on the war room. If it is not already on a Post-It, the item under discussion should be written on a Post-It and placed on the Parking Lot. Make sure to briefly explain the concept of the Parking Lot, and get back to the current activity. It is important to send a strong message to the participants about the Lean Inception: "The conversation is getting off track, and it is not in the current activity scope."

Nevertheless, it is equally important to listen to and respect people's thoughts and feelings. Therefore, the Parking Lot must be used with a pure intention, and be revisited later: "This is parked for now; but we will get back to it later."

Indeed, at the end of each Inception day, you should take ten minutes to review the items in the Parking Lot. Then one of these two actions is taken for each item: 1- The item is removed from the Parking Lot (the topic was already covered or it no longer needs to be addressed), or 2- the item will remain in the Parking Lot for the next review.

The last Parking Lot review should happen towards the end of the Inception. At this last review it is very important to clarify any remaining items and share what will happen to it with everyone.

THE AGENDAS

THE BURN-UP AGENDA

The burn-up agenda helps track the progress of a Lean Inception workshop. Having the agenda visible to everyone builds up the group confidence and awareness towards time management and the progress of activities as a whole. It is a simple and effective tool to plan and facilitate the Lean Inception workshop.

> Burn-up agendas[7] emerged from intensive brainstorming workshops, such as inceptions and ideations. Even though such workshops invite broad discussion, typically they have a time box and must cover a few topics, achieving the desired outcome.

Lean Inception is a collaborative workshop with brainstorming sessions and lots of conversation, that usually takes place in the course of a week. Therefore, it is essential to control its timing and progress. Typically, facilitators create and explain the burn-up agenda in the early hours of the first day of the Lean Inception workshop.

---

7 Read more about burn-up agenda at: <www.caroli.org/en/burn-up-agenda>. Access in: Jul. 2019.

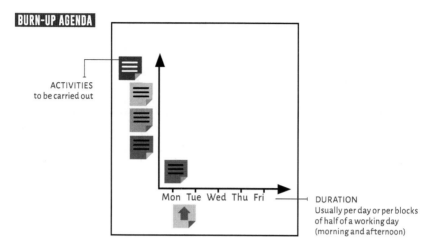

BURN-UP AGENDA

ACTIVITIES
to be carried out

Mon Tue Wed Thu Fri

DURATION
Usually per day or per blocks
of half of a working day
(morning and afternoon)

Here is the step-by-step to create the Lean Inception's burn-up agenda:

1. Draw on a whiteboard or an A3 sheet an XY chart as shown above.

2. Write down in separate Post-Its the activities for your Lean Inception (for instance: product view, Is - Is not - Does - Does not do, personas, feature brainstorming, review, journeys, sequencer, and MVP canvas).

3. Put the activities from the bottom up on the Y axis (first Product vision, followed by Is – Is not – Does – Does not do, and so on)

4. Create Post-Its for the time blocks of your Lean Inception (as it usually lasts a week, the blocks are typically defined as: Monday morning, Monday afternoon, Tuesday morning, etc.).

5. Place the time blocks Post-Its on the Y axis.

6. Draw an arrow (vertical, up) on another Post-It and place it at the beginning of duration (Monday morning).

7. Explain to the group how to use the burn-up agenda.

The burn-up agenda poster and other useful posters for your Lean Inception workshop are available at: **www.caroli.org/en/lean-inception-posters/**.

> There are two basic movements for the Post-Its on the burn-up agenda, and both are horizontal movements: 1- To update the "clock": the Post-It with the arrow representing the current time must be moved to the right to the position representing the current time; 2- to indicate the end of an activity: the respective activity Post-It should be moved to the right, to the position representing the current time.

The Post-It moving mechanism allows everyone to identify a detour in the expected progress for the Lean Inception activities. In such case, the participants should talk about the time tracking challenge and possible corrective actions (parallelizing activities, reducing conversations, making more use of parking lot, etc.). The good thing: such conversation takes place at an early stage, not when it is too late.

THE WEEK AGENDA

The burn-up agenda provides a good framework for sequencing open brainstorming sessions and activities while tracking the overall progress and the time. However, some people, especially those who won't be dedicated to the Inception workshop, need to have an overall view of the week. For that reason I share the planned Lean Inception agenda (available at **www.caroli.org/en/lean-inception-agenda-template/**).

LEAN INCEPTION - TIMETABLE EXAMPLE

	MONDAY	TUESDAY	WEDNESDAY	THURSDAY	FRIDAY
MORNING	LEAN INCEPTION KICK-OFF / WRITE THE PRODUCT VISION	DESCRIBE THE PERSONAS	TECHNICAL, UX, AND BUSINESS REVIEW	BUILD THE FEATURES SEQUENCER	LEAN INCEPTION SHOWCASE
	LUNCH BREAK				
AFTERNOON	PRODUCT IS/-ISN'T-DOES-DOESN'T DO	FEATURES BRAINSTORM	SHOW USERS' JOURNEYS	FILL IN THE MVP CANVAS	

The model of planned agenda with fixed time slots presents two types of sessions (represented by two colors) that correspond to the levels of participation: stakeholders or active members.

» Stakeholder is anyone impacted by the project. These are people very much interested in the direction and result of the Inception, but they do not have the time to attend all sessions. These can include: sponsors, final users, legal department, sales department, and marketing department.

» Active member is anyone directly involved in the understanding and implementation of the product. These are the people who should participate actively in every session of the workshop. They can be: product owners, developers, testers, project manager, and user experience.

Notice that in the planned agenda the kick-off activities and the workshop showcase are marked in a specific color, respectively, in the beginning

THE **BURN-UP AGENDA** HELPS TRACK THE PROGRESS OF A LEAN INCEPTION WORKSHOP. HAVING THE AGENDA VISIBLE TO EVERYONE **BUILDS UP THE GROUP CONFIDENCE AND AWARENESS** TOWARDS TIME MANAGEMENT AND THE PROGRESS OF ACTIVITIES AS A WHOLE.

and in the end of the week. In an ideal world, everyone would be present in the war room during the week. However, we rarely have free schedule time from stakeholders. The minimum necessary is that the stakeholders attend the kick-off and showcase sessions, in which the business expectations for the Inception workshop are presented, as well as the results obtained by the team in the workshop. The other days are taken by a sequence of intense activities, followed by consolidation periods.

THE INCEPTION PLANNING CHECKLIST

The following checklist is designed to aid the Inception planning process. Please make sure to have all items scheduled before starting an Inception.

( ) Participants selected and invited (stakeholders and active members).

( ) Experienced facilitator.

( ) Booking of the room (keep the same room allocated for the entire Inception period).

( ) Materials: Flip chart, index-cards, colored Post-Its, A4 paper and pens for everyone.

( ) Coffee break.

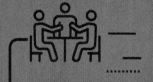

LEAN INCEPTION
ACTIVITIES

WRITE THE PRODUCT VISION

With a good understanding of the product vision, you can determine which are the first pieces of your business puzzle and how they are going to come together. You must decide which product feature the initial path is going to trace and what your strategy is going to be.

Somewhere between the idea and the launching, the vision of the product helps to trace the initial path. It defines the essence of your business value and must convey a clear and convincing message to clients. This activity will help you define collaboratively the vision of the product.

PRODUCT VISION TEMPLATE[8]

For: [final client],

Whose: [problem that needs to be solved].

The: [name of the product]

is a: [product category]

that: [key-benefits, reason to buy it],

different from: [competition or current alternative].

Our product is: [key-difference].

---

8 MOORE, Geoffrey. Template "The vision of the product", described in the book *Crossing the Chasm: Marketing and selling disruptive products to mainstream customers*, HarperBusiness, 2014.

ACTIVITY STEP BY STEP

1. Write the template of the product vision on a whiteboard or flipchart in a visible way for the whole team.
2. Divide the team into smaller groups and ask each group to fill in a blank separately (or more than one, depending on the size of the team).
3. Gather the results of each group, forming a unique sentence.

In this activity it is very common for the result to be a senseless sentence. So, after executing the third step, it is important that the team works together to form a homogeneous sentence, using and altering the previous results, if necessary.

THE PRODUCT IS – IS NOT – DOES – DOES NOT DO

Sometimes, it's easier to describe something by telling what this thing is not or does not do. The activity Is – Is not – Does – Does not do (or INDND) seeks to explain the product this way, asking questions specifically about each positive and negative aspect of the product and what it is or what it does.

ACTIVITY STEP BY STEP

1. Divide a white canvas or flipchart into four areas (Is / Is not / Does / Does not do).
2. Write the name of the product above each quadrant.
3. Ask each participant to describe the product on Post-Its and put them in the corresponding areas.
4. Read and gather similar notes.

The product is...

The product is not...

The product does...

The product does not do...

OUR PRODUCT

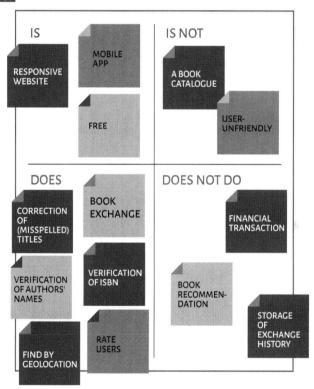

This activity helps to explain the product. Afterwards, the participants usually have a more coordinated view regarding what the product does, as well as what the product doesn't do. Strategic decisions can be clarified, such as something the product will never do, while that other one it still wouldn't do.

> **TIP:** Once, in a workshop, I was asked the difference between "Is" and "Does." A participant— Aurineide Cavalcante—gave a simple and effective answer: "To describe the product as a noun or adjective, put the Post-It in the 'is'; but if it is a verb, indicating an action, put it on the 'Does' category." For example: "secure" and "mobile application" are in the "Is" quadrant, "connect players" and "write msg on chat" are in the "Does" quadrant.

I learned this activity from Rafael Sabbagh, when he used it to define one of the roles of Scrum during his trainings. I adapted this activity to help define the product, and have had excellent results with it.

CLEARING THE OBJECTIVE

Each team member must share what is his/her understanding of the product objectives, and the several points of view must be discussed in order to reach a consensus on what is really important. This activity helps raise and clarify these objectives.

ACTIVITY STEP BY STEP

1. Ask each team member to write, individually, three answers to the following question: "If you had to define this product with three objectives for its users, which would they be?"

2. Ask the participants to share what they wrote on a common canvas, grouping them by similarity.

3. Ask the team to rewrite the objectives, now collectively, and list them in order of importance. By this time, it will be clear that some of the goals

listed do not really represent the main priority of the product, and must be delayed (or discarded). This way it will be clear to the team what is the focus of this product.

UNDERSTANDING TRADE-OFFS

Trade-off is a trade in which you let something go in order to get something else you want more. A lean product reflects decisions of the team regarding trade-offs.

The activity "Understanding trade-offs" helps to build and record a common understanding about trade-offs of the lean product. Many decisions and conversations are based on individual visions and premises between choices. Some examples: What is most valuable: security or usability? What about performance *versus* security? Usability *versus* performance? This activity promotes an open and collaborative conversation on trade-offs. Clearer trade-offs avoid misunderstandings and help to make decisions quickly.

ACTIVITY STEP BY STEP

1. Describe all categories that are relevant to the product on Post-Its (for instance: security, usability, scalability).

2. Write the categories on the white board or on the flipchart as row titles. Then, draw a horizontal line under each category.

3. Draw vertical lines (the same number as the horizontal lines).

4. Write "more" (important) above the line to the left and "less" above the line to the right.

5. Ask participants to write their initials in several Post-Its and put one Post-It on each line. The restriction: each column must contain a Post-It

with your initials (for example: only one of the categories will be marked as more important).

6. Equalize the trade-offs. With a Post-It of a different color (dark blue Post-Its in the next image), set the markings for each category, from less important to most important. This marking should be relatively easy since it considers the Post-Its with the votes of everyone.

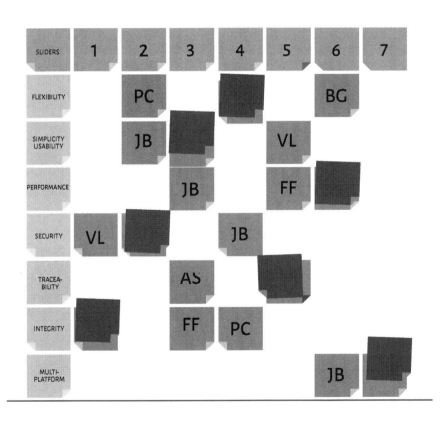

DESCRIBE THE PERSONAS

To effectively identify the functionalities of a product, it is important to bear in mind users and their goals. The path usually chosen is to represent these users through personas.

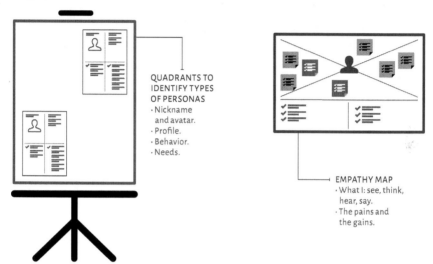

QUADRANTS TO IDENTIFY TYPES OF PERSONAS
· Nickname and avatar.
· Profile.
· Behavior.
· Needs.

EMPATHY MAP
· What I: see, think, hear, say.
· The pains and the gains.

A persona represents a user in the system, describing not only his or her role but also his or her specific needs, creating a realistic representation of users, helping the team to describe functionalities from the point of view of those who will interact with the final product.

QUADRANTS TO IDENTIFY TYPES OF PERSONAS

The following activity is used to describe the types of personas. This is a simple, illustrative, fun and quick activity.

ACTIVITY STEP BY STEP

1. Divide the team into pairs or triplets and hand the following template of personas to each group.

TO EFFECTIVELY
IDENTIFY THE
FUNCTIONALITIES
OF A PRODUCT, IT IS
IMPORTANT TO BEAR
IN MIND USERS AND
THEIR GOALS.

Nickname and avatar	Profile · · · · · · ·
Behavior · · · · · ·	Needs · · · · ·

2. Ask each group to create a persona, using the template as reference.

3. Ask participants to present their personas for the whole team.

4. Ask the team to change groups and repeat steps 1 to 3.

The template presented was created by Natalia Arsand, an excellent User eXperience designer and a colleague at ThoughtWorks Brasil.

By the end of the activity, a set of personas will have been created and the different types of product users will have been described. The stakeholders who know the goals of the product must participate actively, helping the team create the personas and suggesting changes in their descriptions, as needed.

CREATING EMPATHY MAPS

The empathy map is a visual template used to identify and visualize a persona. It was originally developed to analyze consumer segments, but empathy mapping is an excellent tool to classify, explore and understand different types of personas.

The empathy map was originally described by Dave Gray as one of the methods used by XPLANE[9] to understand users, clients, and other participants in

9 XPLANE is a visual thinking company founded in 1993 by Dave Gray.

the business. It became more widely known since it was presented in the book *Business Model Generation* as a tool to discover insights on clients.

The map contains four main areas, which fulfill the sentence:

WHAT DO I _____ (SEE / THINK / HEAR / SAY)?

Aside from these four main areas, the original version presents two more fields: pain and gain, for each persona.

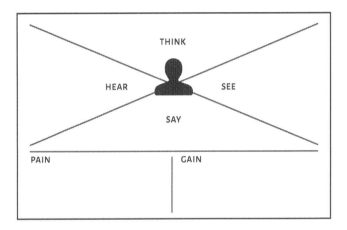

Every time I've applied the Empathy Map for persona identification, I've used its four main areas: see, hear, think, and say. Sometimes, I use the pain and gain areas, as described originally; but other times I change these two areas, for instance: what I do, what I don't do, my friends and my enemies, my hobbies.

ACTIVITY STEP BY STEP

1. Choose a persona to be analyzed.
2. Draw a template of the map, putting the persona in the center.
3. Describe the areas for such persona.

4. Repeat steps 2 and 3 for the next personas.

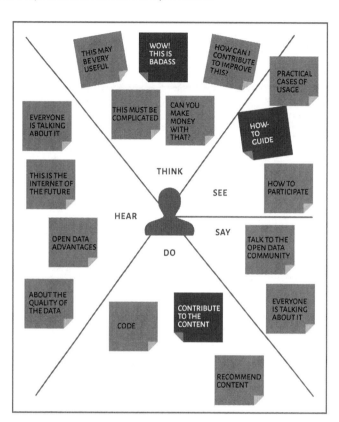

UPDATE THE PERSONA DESCRIPTION

The "Describing personas" activity does generate a few pieces of information detailing the current understanding of each persona. But it is important to emphasize that such understanding should not be considered definitive, but an initial construction that can and should be updated as the product evolves.

The activity is based on knowledge, research, and preliminary data about the product users. Generally, organizations with established products have knowledge and data about their users. If this is not the case, a portion of the business hypotheses is dedicated to the users of the product: will we reach the desired users with this MVP?

Based on the MVP usage data, we get more understanding about the personas, the people using it. In addition, more research can be done to obtain more information about the users. As more knowledge is obtained, you should revisit the "describing personas" activity, updating the representation of the users.

Samantha Rosa, a User eXperience consultant, shared an example of this. During a Lean Inception, her team followed the steps of the activity and created the personas, but after making the product available to real customers, they realized that one of the personas described was not in accordance with reality. So her team updated the information about the persona and redesigned a few of the related product features.

FEATURE BRAINSTORMING

Feature is the description of an action or interaction of a user with the product. For example: print invoice, see detailed statement, and invite Facebook friends.

The description of a feature should be as simple as possible. The user is trying to do something. The product should have a feature for that. What is the feature?

Since you already described the personas and the main business goals, the following questions help unveil the features:

 What should the product offer in order to meet this person's need? What functionality should we build to achieve this business goal?

The following activity is used to discover features. Note that this activity depends on the list of goals and personas, which must be pieces of information acquired in previous activities.

ACTIVITY STEP BY STEP

1. Ask the team to put the goals on a common canvas, in order of priority, from left to right, as column titles.

2. Ask the team to put the personas on a common canvas, in order of priority, from top to bottom, as row titles.

3. Promote a features brainstorm. The discussion must be guided in order to reveal which features are necessary to reach the goals and personas. The previously showed questions will help you.

The team must guide itself through the canvas, repeating the questions above for every combination of persona and goal, starting with the highest prioritized ones. Thereby, the features with the highest priority will come first.

This book mainly describes my experience with Lean Inceptions for digital products. So I named this activity "Feature brainstorming," because of digital product or MVP features. But in some instances, I explicitly change the name of the activity, from "Feature brainstorming" to: "Activity brainstorming," or "Idea brainstorming." This happens when the context of the Lean Inception is not for the creation of a digital product, but for the alignment of people to build something (not necessarily a product).

SHOW ME THE MONEY

Time tracking is essential for all activities, but this one requires special attention. In case a great number of goals and personas are selected (in steps 1 and 2), numerous features might be raised by the team. This will not be productive and can lead the team to spend too much time debating funcionalities that will not be in the first MVPs.

In order to avoid such a scenario, it is strongly recommended that the number of goals and personas are shortened to very few (such as the top three or four each).

 If we were on a very short budget and could work on only one goal, which would that be?

The question above helps the group to prioritize goals and personas. Repeat it a few times for goals, then for personas. This should help with prioritization and focused discussions towards a product MVP.

A more playful and collaborative way of prioritizing goals and/ or personas is thinking about money. With this intent, propose the following activity:

ACTIVITY STEP BY STEP

1. Divide the participants into smaller groups.
2. Pass around five Post-Its with "$" to each group (use one color of Post-It per group).
3. Instruct the group to place the "$" where they believe more money should be invested (either in better understanding the persona's need or in achieving that goal).
4. Discuss the outcome (give the option of redistributing the "$").
5. Prioritize items with more "$".

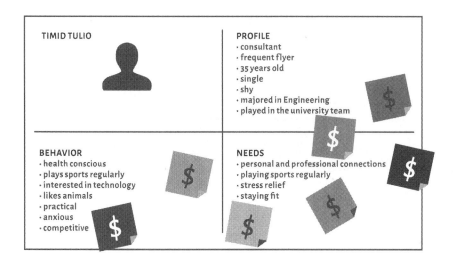

FEATURES, GOALS, AND PERSONAS

Although the canvas is similar to a table, there will not necessarily be a feature for each intersection. There may be multiple features for a persona and a specific goal, just as there may be personas that do not need a feature for a particular goal. Also, some features might fit more than one persona and one goal.

If a feature does not meet the need of any persona, it should be discarded or reconsidered because their value is not clearly associated with a user.

TECHNICAL, USER EXPERIENCE AND BUSINESS REVIEW

The brainstorming activity listed many features, but we need to spend more time trying to understand the features in more detail. In order to develop this understanding, we assess the features in terms of effort, business value, user experience, and uncertainty about what it is and how to build it.

For effort, business value, and user experience, we evaluate the features using marks on a scale of one, two, or three.

EFFORT	E	EE	EEE
BUSINESS	$	$$	$$$
UX	♡	♡♡	♡♡♡

Ranking uncertainty is a little trickier.

"I know exactly what I want and I know exactly how to do it." It's amazing when this happens! However, it is not always so. That's why you need to check the level of uncertainty for each feature. The **traffic light** chart will help you do this.

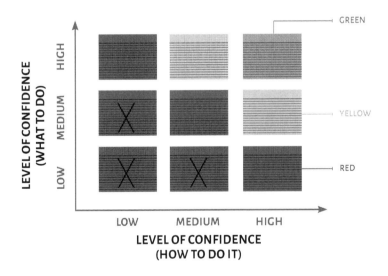

We rate a feature for its technical certainty (how well the development team understands **how to** build the feature) and its business and usage certainty (how well the User eXperience and the business people agree on **what**

goes into the feature). Then we use these two ratings and combine them using the traffic light chart in order to come up with an overall level of uncertainty: red (high), yellow (medium), and green (low). If a feature falls into the lower left part of the table (marked with an "X"), consider discarding it or spending more time clarifying it.

This graphic is named "traffic light chart" because its colors are the same as a traffic light: green, you can move on; yellow, pay attention, you may have to stop before proceeding; red, stop and wait (further investigation) before proceeding.

Upon completion of the technical, User eXperience, and business review, all features will be colored and marked. So for the feature "estimate price", there can be medium effort, low user experience value, high business value, and medium uncertainty.

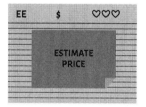

Every single feature should go through technical, UX, and business review. In order to do that, each feature must be plotted on the traffic light chart, and, soon after, should be assessed according to the Effort, User eXperience and Business Value table.

In the chart the feature gets a color; on the table, the feature gets three marks. The color represents the feature's uncertainty level: red for a high level of uncertainty, yellow for a medium level of uncertainty, and green for a low level of uncertainty. The marks deal with effort, business value and UX value, and vary on a scale of one, two or three times in comparison to each other; for example $, $$, and $$$. These color and marks will help the team to prioritize, estimate and plan in subsequent activities.

Below we can see one example of features before and after undergoing both activities.

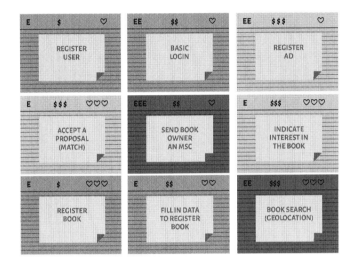

The process of taking each feature through the review generates much more than the colors and the markings on each card. Important technical conversations about the feature take place, such as: architecture, cross-functional requirements, and complexity. Assumptions are verified. Uncertainties are described. As usual with this kind of activity, the conversation and the understanding it generates for those taking part matter more than the final output.

Many of these notes contain extra information about the feature that may be needed later. These might be important, and we don't want to lose them, so we write everything down about the feature on Post-Its, and then stick them behind the index card.

FEATURES IN THE TRAFFIC LIGHT CHART

This activity is aimed at discussing how the team feels in terms of technical, UX, and business certainty for each feature. From this activity, new notes are taken, and disagreements and doubts become more evident.

ACTIVITY STEP BY STEP

1. Create a common canvas, the traffic light chart[10] in which the X axis represents the technical certainty (**how to** do it) and the Y axis represents User eXperience and business agreement to the requirement (**what** to do).

2. Ask a member of the team to read a feature out loud and put it on the graph according to his/her understanding of it (technical certainty and business agreement).

---

10 The traffic light chart poster and other useful posters for your Lean Inception workshop are available at: <www.caroli.org/en/lean-inception-posters/>. Access: Jul. 2019.

- ‣ X axis: How confident are you on how to build this feature?
- ‣ Y axis: How confident are you on what the business and/or the users want from this feature?

3. Check if everyone in the team shares the same opinion. If somebody disagrees, the team must discuss the requirements and the technology involved so that an agreement about the feature is reached. Everything mentioned that helps to achieve a better understanding must be written down and attached to the feature.

4. Take notes about the level of uncertainty on the feature. For instance, the image below shows features on Post-Its that were attached to green (■), yellow (■) or red (■)index cards, indicating low, medium or high uncertainty levels, respectively.

5. For each feature selected previously, repeat steps 2 to 4.

On the X axis, the goal is to verify the team's understanding of technical challenges, dependencies, and infrastructure requirements. Have you done this before? Do you know **how** to do it? "Yes" indicates a high level of confidence on how to do it. "More or less," "maybe" or "I think so" indicate medium level; while "no" indicates low level.

On the Y axis, the idea is to verify the clarity **of what** to build, both from the business point of view and from the usability point of view. Do you know **what** the business and/or the user want from this feature? "Yes" indicates a high level of confidence in **what** to do; "More or less," "maybe" or "I think so" indicate medium level; while "no" indicates low level.

By the end of this activity, all features are categorized according to the technical, UX and business certainty level. Each feature Post-It is placed on a colored index card—green, yellow or red, representing high, medium, and low levels of certainty, respectively.

At the end of the activity, red-card features marked with an X pose very high risks to the project. Typically, the team breaks them into smaller pieces of work or discards them. Avoid them at all costs. Try to clarify them before starting to work.

FEATURES ON THE EFFORT, USER EXPERIENCE AND BUSINESS VALUE TABLE

The goal in this activity is to discuss how the team understands the effort to complete the feature, as well as the business value and the user experience related to it. From this activity, new markings are added to each feature.

ACTIVITY STEP BY STEP

1. Create a table, showing the markings on a scale of one two or three for technical effort (the level of the work that needs to be done), User eXperience value (how much the users will love it) and business value (what is the return or saving that it will bring).

2. Ask a member of the team to read a feature out loud and write it down on each table row according to his/her understanding of it (effort, User eXperience and value to the business).

   ► How much work (effort) will it take to create this feature? Mark E, EE or EEE, indicating low, medium or high.

   ► How much business value will we generate with this feature? Mark $, $$, or $$$, indicating low, medium, or high.

   ► How much will users love this feature? Mark with one, two or three hearts, indicating low, medium or high approval.

3. Ask if everyone in the team shares the same opinion. If anyone disagrees, the team must discuss the requirements and the technology involved so that an agreement is reached about the feature. Everything mentioned that helps to achieve a better understanding must be written down and attached to the feature card.

4. Write down the level of effort, User eXperience and the business value on the feature card.

5. For each feature selected previously, repeat steps 2 to 4.

THE BUSINESS VALUE SCALE

The markings $, $$ and $$$ indicate high value, really high value or super high value in business terms. When I started using this table, these markings were used to indicate high, medium or low business value. But hardly any business person would grade a feature as low value. The change on the scale made it a little easier to assess and compare business value.

In the technical effort conversation, the goal is to verify the understanding of the team according to the difficulty and the work that is going to be involved in completing such feature. In the business value conversation, the proposal is to verify the value, the ROI (Return On Investment) of the feature, a business measurement on how much such a feature is worth. In the User eXperience conversation, the idea is to verify how much the users expect or will love a feature. Such markings represent how the team perceives a feature value or effort in relation to each other.

SHOW THE USERS' JOURNEYS

The user journey describes a sequence of steps a user follows in order to reach a goal. Some of these steps represent points of contact with a product, demonstrating how the user interacts with it. As we build the journey, the team raises questions and alternative opinions about the user's needs and the product features.

ACTIVITY STEP BY STEP

1. Select a persona.
2. Identify a goal for this persona.
3. Write the persona and their goal on a Post-It and place it on the top left side of a canvas (A3 paper or a flipchart are best, since they can be moved around).
4. Decide the starting point (helpful questions: how does the persona start his/her day? What triggers his/her desire to achieve the goal?), write this starting point on a Post-It and put it on the canvas.
5. Describe each of the next steps on a Post-It and place it next on the canvas. Continue placing steps until the persona achieves her goal

Questions, agreements, and disagreements will lead the talk to the building of the journey. Maybe, more than one option of journey will rise. For instance, the optimistic journey, the realistic journey, the pessimistic, the master, the exceptional journey, depending on various factors. The options will force the prioritizing and clear definition of the goal and, as a result, the focus will be clearer in some journeys. The prioritized journeys will complement and help the search for the MVP.

The level of detailing of a journey should be neither too high nor too low. While a journey shows a step-by-step guide of the user's interaction, it is also a synthesis, a simplified and higher level of the flow without the redundant information and the deeper details.

Below is a sample of a user journey. Note the stickman drawing (representing a persona whose nickname is Dick) next to a car on the top left-hand side of the sheet, and his journey described with many Post-Its from left to right, from top to bottom. In this journey, each Post-It indicates one step of the path towards reaching his/her goal (described in the last Post-It). Small arrows were marked connecting one step to the next.

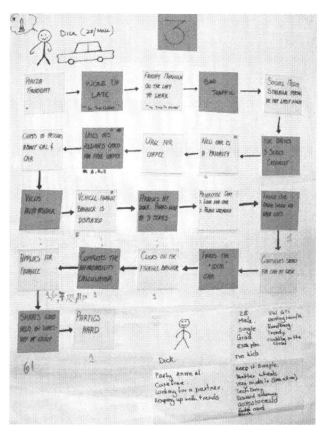

Simple questions help the beginning of the journey description. Here are some examples:

Which goal does this persona want to reach? How does he or she start the day? What does he/she do before this? What does he/she do after this?

A conversation, a Post-It, and a pen. This is what you need to describe the journey of a user. I suggest writing and rewriting. But get started, don't stand still waiting for an insight that won't come. After having written some stuff down, you can change it. If it makes sense, combine some detailed steps into one. Or break up a very detailed step into smaller ones. There is no magic to it. The important thing is that the journeys are described.

Here is an example of a user journey:

SOCCER FAN: INVITE FRIENDS TO A GAME

- Wakes up early to work.
- Has a big breakfast.
- Arrives at work at 9:00 a.m.
- During a meeting, decides he needs some physical activity
- At lunch, talks a friend into playing soccer after work.
- Calls and books a field.
- Opens Easy-bola mobile app.
- Sets the match for 8:00 p.m. that evening.
- Fills in the information about the field he booked.
- Sends invitation to friends.

DISPLAY FEATURES IN THE JOURNEYS

Journeys clarify what the interaction with the product will be like. If you've followed the order depicted in this book, the journeys must be described (like a sequence of steps on a table or a canvas) and the features must be available (in single index cards). This activity describes how to put them together, revalidating and verifying the entire analysis up to this moment.

ACTIVITY STEP BY STEP

1. Divide participants into two groups, one should be close to the journeys, and the other close to the features.

2. Ask someone in the journey group to slowly read the step-by-step of the user's journey.

3. As a person reads the journey step by step, the people in the feature group check to see if there is any feature that meets or enhances the user's journey.

4. When a "match" is identified (from a feature on the journey), give the feature an ID, write it down on a small Post-It, and place it on the journey step.

5. Repeat the previous steps for all journeys.

While one person is reading the user's journey, the others must be looking for the features they need. The team can use a numeric identifier for each feature (for example: 1, 2, 3, 28, 32). Write down the number on the journey feature card and on a small Post-It. Attach it to the journey, on the step the persona would take.

The next image brings yet another example for mapping features on a journey. When this photo was taken, one person was reading the user's journey,

THE **USER JOURNEY** DESCRIBES A **SEQUENCE** OF STEPS A USER FOLLOWS IN ORDER TO REACH A GOAL.

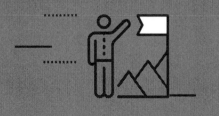

while three other people were looking for features used on this journey. Small Post-Its with features identifiers (e.g. 29, 30, 31, 32) were added.

By the end of this activity, two things might occur: (1) missing features are identified for some journeys, and (2) some features were not mapped in any journeys.

For the former situation you must create the feature cards as according to the colors and markings identifying uncertainty, effort, and value. The latter is an indication that some features are not mapped for the users' journeys. These features should be cleared up (and documented), but the team does not need to carry them forward, keeping the focus on priority items, according to the main journeys.

SEQUENCE THE FEATURES

"Is this feature important?" I've always got the same answer when asking such question. That is why I don't ask it anymore. The most relevant question that will help you plan the order of the features to be created is: "Which one of these two is the priority?"

So the features are prioritized according to one another. This question is very useful and must be asked, but from as a starting point.

Previously, you identified the most important persona, as well as the highest priority journey. That is for sure the best starting point: the first feature of this journey.

Maybe more than one feature will be in the journey, or in journeys that can be created at the same time. In such scenario, you must ask which one of the two features has the highest priority.

Fortunately, in the previous stages some parameters have already been added to the features. They are: business value ($, $$ or $$$), user experience (one, two, or three hearts), effort (E, EE or EEE), and uncertainty level (green, yellow or red card, identifying high, medium or low uncertainty, respectively). These parameters will help you with the planning of features and their relative priorities.

 So, what is the minimum combination of features that can be available to validate a small set of hypotheses of the business?

Now it is time to visualize and conceptualize the first MVP and its following increments. For this, use the feature sequencer.

THE FEATURE SEQUENCER

The purpose of a minimum viable product is to create something that you can use to validate a small set of assumptions about a product and its role in a business. Now that you have a mapping of features integrated and user journeys, you are in a position to work out the MVP and its following iterations. You do this by defining a features sequencer.

ACTIVITY STEP BY STEP

1. Create the feature sequencer template (typically a flipchart with numbered lines; the line height should fit one feature card, the line width should fit three feature cards).
2. Explain the rules of the feature sequencer.
3. Remind everyone about the activity goal: To define the sequence in which the features of the product will be delivered.
4. Everyone places the feature cards on the sequencer, moving them around as the group explores the options, until they reach an agreement.
5. The result shows the features for the MVP and its following iterations.

 Our goal with an MVP is to learn from each iteration by building something that will allow us to test if our business case is effective.

THE FEATURE SEQUENCER WAVES

You must plan a sequence of waves for grouping features in order to help you organize the production order, something easy to understand. A wave after another, in sequence. Draw on a flipchart or white board a template with the waves, the feature sequencer.

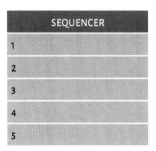

The purpose: To build the MVP features as early as possible. And continue working on the sequencer's features, from wave to wave, adding features to the product and the business strategy. To help decide what to put on which wave and in which order, follow the rules of the sequencer.

THE RULES FOR EACH WAVE

Features will be added to each wave. These are the rules for adding features to the waves. These rules were defined after applying this type of planning and prioritizing countless times.

- » **Rule 1:** A wave can contain a maximum of three features.
- » **Rule 2:** A wave cannot contain more than one feature with a red card (high uncertainty).
- » **Rule 3:** A wave cannot contain three features only on yellow or red cards.
- » **Rule 4:** The effort score of the features cannot add up to more than 5 Es per wave.
- » **Rule 5:** The sum of the value of the features cannot be less than four "$" and four hearts.

» **Rule 6:** If one feature depends on another, that other must be on some previous wave.

I came up with these rules after running many lean inceptions, and I consider them a good way to guide the iterative construction of the MVP.

Rule 1 limits the number of features being worked on at the same time. This avoids the accumulation of partially completed work items, increasing the focus to the few prioritized features. Rules 2, 3 and 4 avoid unbalanced working periods, with too much uncertainty or too much effort. Rule 5 ensures a constant focus on delivering high value to the business and the users. Rule 6 avoids dependency issues between features.

CONVERGING RULES AND JOURNEYS

Simple rules are added to the Feature Sequencer template. Now, it's just a matter of selecting the first features of the first journey. Then you must select the next one. By respecting the rules, you will decide if such feature gets in the wave "n" or "n+1."

If in doubt between two features that are in compliance with the rules, just answer the question "Which one has the highest priority?"

Below, you see an image that will exemplify how to put the feature in a wave of the template, respecting the rules.

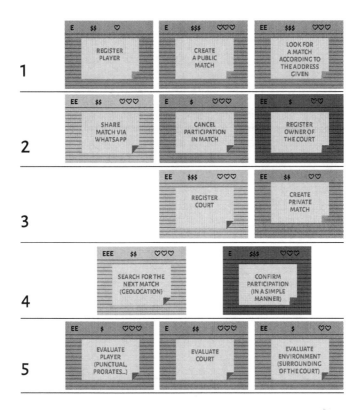

DUPLICATE OR USE THE SAME POST-IT OR CARD?

A feature with its markings is positioned on a canvas (for example, a journey canvas). You are about to take the card and place it on another canvas: the Feature Sequencer. In addition to the information described in the card, its position on the canvas contains more information. This is the case of the feature with the journey and on the Feature Sequencer. At this time you will ask: Do I duplicate it or use the same card? My suggestion is: take a picture before anything else. Then consider replicating the card, as long as it doesn't make the activity slower and the environment more confused (with the innumerous colored papers).

Typically, the Lean Inception participants are very active while using the feature sequencer. At this point everyone is well aligned regarding the main journeys and their features (with their markings of uncertainty level, business value, UX value, and effort). A common setting is: everyone standing in front of the sequencer, with cards on their hands, having conversations and moving cards around, depicting different options and strategies.

IDENTIFYING MVPS IN THE FEATURE SEQUENCER

Now it is the time to understand the increments and the evolutionary creation of your product. The activities so far have cleared up and prioritized each aspect of your product.

The small blocks of the product, the features, are now arranged logically in the feature sequencer. In addition, you understand them and visualize them for the users' journeys. By browsing the flipchart of the feature sequencer with its waves and features, you will elucidate the MVP increments.

Whenever the combination of features reaches a simple version of the product that can become available, call it: MVP. Below, there is one example after the stage of identifying MVPs.

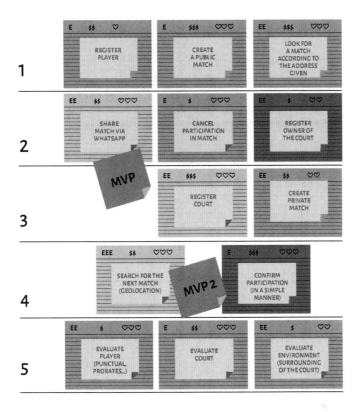

The waves won't necessary relate one-to-one with the MVPs. Note that this was the case in the examples of MVP on the feature sequencer presented previously. The intention is to practice planning and sequencing features in waves in order to deliver value as fast as possible, while respecting the dependencies between features and the rules of feature sequencer.

Below is an illustrative example for a Feature Sequencer. In it you will find two MVPs and thirteen features. MVP 1 is composed of the features F1 to F5. MVP 2 is composed of features F6 to F12.

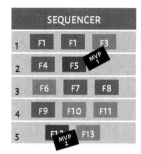

What do I mean by MVP2? You already identified the MVP as the minimum viable product, so afterwards, there will be increments to the product. Whether you call the next increment MVP 2 or some other name, the most important thing is that you continue to increment your product-based learning and hypotheses validation: build-measure-learn.

CALCULATING EFFORT, TIME AND COST

Most of the enterprises I know are very interested in answering two simple and direct questions: What are you building? And when will it be done?

The features sequencer answers the first question. It shows the MVP and its following iterations. It is an awesome artifact generated at your Lean Inception. Many stakeholders will be really satisfied when you answer such an important question.

But when is it done? Some people will ask you this. When is the MVP going to be ready? And the next one? What about all of those features on the features sequencer?

If this is not your case, you are lucky and can skip this chapter; otherwise, in this chapter, I'll share how I have been helping many teams answer such questions.

The sequence of activities up to this moment, as well as the rules of the feature sequencer generate waves similar in size. This simplifies the estimation of the product with its MVPs, as it provides the means to work with an average wave size based on a smaller sampling. Instead of detailing every wave with its features according to effort, time, and cost, you will select only a few waves. Then you will detail its features, add up the numbers and calculate the average for a wave.

DETAILING SAMPLE FEATURES INTO TASKS

The size of the waves is similar. So pick two or three waves and use them to generate detailed information on effort, time and cost. Two or three waves are enough to give you a good view on such parameters and generate an effective average.

ACTIVITY STEP BY STEP

1. Pick two or three sample waves to be detailed.
2. Select a feature of one of the sample waves.
3. Describe, on other cards, the smaller tasks for the selected feature.
4. Go back to step 2 and select another feature until you have detailed all features of the sample waves.

When selecting the sample waves (step 1), remember that at this point you are interested in the estimate of the whole and the average size of a wave, and not in detailing the work itself. Therefore, the waves to be chosen must provide a good combination of the uncertainty level (marked by the colors of the features cards).

MOST OF THE ENTERPRISES I KNOW ARE VERY INTERESTED IN ANSWERING TWO SIMPLE AND DIRECT QUESTIONS: WHAT ARE YOU BUILDING? AND WHEN WILL IT BE DONE?

The smaller piece (step 3) must be something that makes sense for each team. Software development teams that follow the Scrum methodology typically pick user stories as those smaller pieces. Other teams prefer to choose the smaller pieces as tasks and describe them with no predefined format.

In the context of this book, I will call the smaller pieces of a feature, "tasks." Typically, I recommend that the teams be very specific while creating these task cards, as this will help the current activity—but not to worry about documenting it perfectly, as this should be done later, and not during the Lean Inception.

During step 3, make identification markings on both the feature card and its task cards. For instance, mark F1 for all tasks from feature 1, F2 for the tasks from feature 2, and so on. This is done to avoid confusion and mixing up the required features and its tasks.

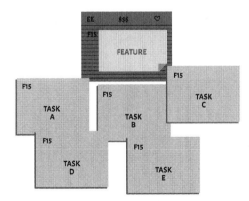

By the end of this activity, the features selected as samples will have been detailed with their several tasks.

SIZING

This activity is very simple but essential to understand the relative effort of tasks.

ACTIVITY STEP BY STEP

1. Write the following T-shirt sizes on Post-Its: small, medium, and large.

2. Place the Post-Its on the canvas (typically a tabletop), small at the top left corner, and large at the bottom left corner.

3. Select two tasks and ask the following question: How does this one task compare (in effort) to this other one? Both small? One small, one medium? Large?

4. Put both tasks on the canvas, with their respective positions indicating how they compare in relation to the effort level (small, medium or large). Place one next to the other, if both required the same effort level; or place one under the other, indicating that one requires more effort than the other.

5. Define the limit between sizes and reposition tasks to make their sizes clear. If needed, consider creating an extra T-shirt size (either XS or XL, for extra-small or extra-large).

6. While there are still tasks to be compared, place them on the canvas according to the effort level and repeat steps 3 and 4.

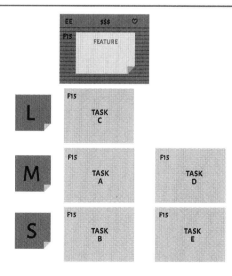

By the end of this activity, each task will be associated to a T-shirt size: small, medium or large.

The previous two activities (detailing sample features into tasks and sizing) can and should be carried at the same time, as depicted in the next image.

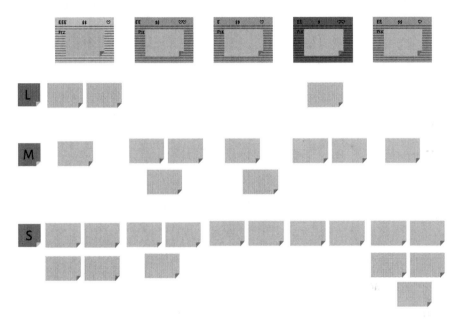

Here, the tasks are placed according to their respective sample feature, and next to tasks of similar size.

UNDERSTANDING COST AND TIME

This activity is essential to generate numbers for calculating cost and time for each wave, as well as for the whole feature sequencer. After it, you will be able to answer the question: When is it done?

ACTIVITY STEP BY STEP

1. Choose a small task and ask how long a person may take to complete it.

2. Choose two or three more tasks of the same size and ask the same question.

3. Calculate the average time and take note.

4. Repeat the previous steps with tasks of different sizes.

By the end of this activity, all tasks will have an estimate of time and cost. For instance, the following result was obtained as a result of this activity: half a day for small tasks, two days for medium tasks, four days for large tasks, and eight days for extra-large tasks.

The answers will influence the final outcome. So be emphatic regarding the questions. If possible, ask for comparisons with past projects, and try to understand the motivation and the ability of people answering such question.

Developers do not like to answer this question: "How long does it take to complete such a task?" Therefore, it is very important that everyone feels very comfortable with the task description. If there is any discomfort in relation to a task, rewrite it, and consider breaking it into smaller pieces.

Another way to ask the question is to put it in the plural:

 Consider a pair of developers. One knows more about the business, the other one knows less. One is a senior, the other one is younger. One is savvier on the specific technology, the other one is a beginner. How long does it take for the pair of developers to complete such a task?

In my experience, everyone is more comfortable giving such an answer considering pairs of developers working together to complete a task.

CALCULATING THE AVERAGE FOR A WAVE

By understanding the effort in the previous activity, we added the estimated time for each task in each feature. Then, we added the estimated time per feature of each line of the sequencer. Then, we reached an average of effort for each line, defined per person per time unit.

Both of the following pictures show how the math was done for a team. The pictures show respectively the waves chosen per sampling and how it was calculated in order to reach the average of the estimated time per wave.

F4	¼ ¼ ½ ½ 2 2	5 ½	12 days
F5	½ ½ ½ ½ ½ 2 2	6 ½	
F6	½ ½ ½	1 ½	
F7	¼ ½ ½ ½ 5	6 ¾	11 ½ days
F8	¼ ½ ½ 2	3 ¼	
F9	¼ ¼ ¼ ½ ½ ½	2 ¼	
F10	¼ ½ ½ ½ 2	3 ¾	9 days for two developers
F11	½ ½ 2	3	

The previous image shows the calculation made to get the average time estimated per wave. Each task was estimated in days for a pair of developers. In the picture, each line shows the entire period estimated per task of a feature. The measure of estimated time for each task was: ¼ of a day (small), ½ day (medium), two days (large) or five days (extra large). Making the sum per feature and then per wave, the team has reached the total of eleven days, eleven and a half days and nine days, respectively, for the waves 2, 3 and 4. The average used for this team was ten days for a pair of developers per wave.

Below you can see another example of outcome for another team.

FEATURE	XS 1 day	S 1 week	M 2 weeks	L 4 weeks		
56	1	1		2	9 weeks, 1 day	
50	1	2			2 weeks, 1 day	14 weeks
13A	2		1		2 weeks, 1 day	
45	2	2			2 weeks, 1 day	
31	1	3			3 weeks, 1 day	9 weeks
33	1	3			3 weeks, 1 day	

The image above shows another Lean Inception result for two selected sample waves: nine weeks, and fourteen weeks. After verifying this activity result, the main stakeholder said: "So, each wave takes approximately twelve weeks for one developer. As we have six developers in this team, it looks like we can deliver a wave every two weeks (twelve developer-weeks divided by six developers), or a wave per Sprint, according to your Scrum terminology." Then he continued: "As our MVP is ready on wave 5... I guess I have to do some adjustment to the planning."

BUILD THE MVP CANVAS

Finally, we hit the apex of the Lean Inception: the MVP Canvas. In it, we are going to detail the MVP and its features regarding the perspectives of **Design Thinking** and **Lean Startup**.

The MVP Canvas was conceived as a Lean Inception activity, and it is the last activity of the Lean Inception workshop. However, it can be used alone regardless of the sequence of the Lean Inception.

But I emphasize that it is very important to align the participants about the product vision, the goals, the personas, the features, the journeys, and the sequence of features comprising each MVP. That helps filling out the MVP Canvas.

One hour: that is approximately how long it takes to fill out the MVP Canvas if you have followed the Lean Inception activities as described in the previous chapters. One hour working at the MVP canvas will get you to a good level of detail and a lot of discussion on each canvas quadrant.

On the other hand, a team that has not followed the Lean Inception step by step will need more time and much more dialogue to create an MVP Canvas.

FILLING OUT THE MVP CANVAS

Considering the team has already discussed what comprises the MVP and has already talked about what they expect from it, it is now time to put everything on paper. Better yet, define the essential thoughts about the MVP in a single piece of paper: the MVP Canvas.

Segmented personas **2**	MVP proposal **1**	Expected outcome **5**
	Features **4**	
Journeys **3**		Metrics to validate the business hypotheses **6**
	Cost and schedule **7**	

ACTIVITY STEP BY STEP

1. Print the MVP Canvas[11] or draw it on a flip chart.

2. Choose the MVP to be developed.

3. Fill out, in a group, each of the seven blocks of the MVP Canvas.

The MVP Canvas is divided into seven sections. The questions to be answered in each one are:

1. **MVP Proposal:** What is the proposal for this MVP?

2. **Segmented personas:** Who is this MVP for? Can we segment and test this MVP in a smaller group?

3. **Journeys:** What journeys are going to be improved by this MVP?

4. **Features:** What are we building in this MVP? Which actions are going to be simplified or improved in this MVP?

5. **Expected result:** What learning or result are we seeking in this MVP?

6. **Metrics to validate the business hypotheses:** How can we measure the results of this MVP?

7. **Cost and schedule:** What is the expected cost and due date for this MVP? Is there any schedule constraint?

THE FEATURE SEQUENCER AND THE MVP CANVAS

The feature sequencer helps the organization and visualization of features. The sequencer organizes and plans product delivery beyond the MVP, clearly depicting the product features release sequence.

---

11 Articl about MVP Canvas (including file to be printed) by Paulo Caroli (2018). Available at <www.caroli.org/en/the-mvp-canvas/>. Access in: Sep. 2018.

Besides displaying the sorted feature cards, the sequencer clearly shows the feature grouping for each MVP. This is represented by Post-Its placed in the sequencer, delimiting the MVP1, the MVP2 and so on.

If you used the feature sequencer and marked one, two or three MVPs on it, I suggest you print three MVP Canvas and fill out one for each MVP identified in the sequencer. However, if you used the sequencer and there are too many MVPs, I also suggest that you print three canvases and only fill out the first three MVPs.

The fact is that we are working with MVPs, and we do not want to go too far. Maybe the feature sequencer has too many features and, while sorting and grouping them, some MVPs may come up. This happens because, in general, the participants of the product inception first think in a broader way and then try to determine the sequence of the minimum and viable deliverables. And the feature sequencer demonstrates clearly the collective thinking about the product evolution via MVPs.

But the sequencer is only a mapping, a plan we create according to current understanding. And this sequence is created assuming that the first MVPs achieve what we are expecting from them. However, don't be fooled. The learning from MVP1 and later from MVP2 will bring some new explanations. The team will have to re-think the product and the next MVPs with their features.

Building an MVP Canvas and putting it in the closet would be a waste. Build one, two, but no more than three versions. The example in the image is real; that team only built one MVP Canvas for the first MVP. Follow their example. Only build a new MVP Canvas when you are close to working on the given MVP, considering the learning you have gathered so far.

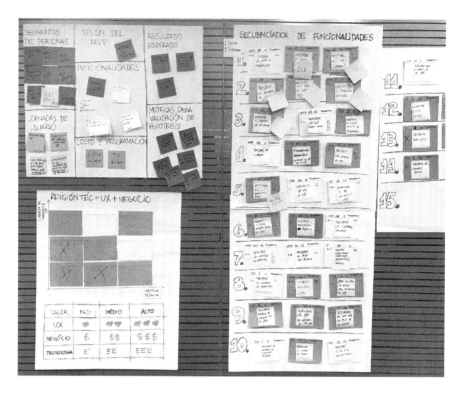

MVP Canvas next to the feature sequencer

FOCUS ON THE PROPOSAL

The more focused the MVP is, the better. It must validate the need for a segment of personas and one hypothesis of the business, and, in general, these are related. However, in some contexts, the MVP is broader than one need and one hypothesis. Whatever your business context is, be clear about the **MVP proposal**.

 Ask yourself until it is crystal clear: What is the proposal of this MVP?

An example of an MVP proposal: To validate if residents of the Ipanema neighborhood will call a taxi via a newly-released website. This proposal is very close to the story of EasyTaxi in 2011: "The application started with an MVP 'concierge.' The founder team provided a webpage for users to enter the address they were at—and a click on the 'Call my taxi' button, which would e-mail one of the founders with the inputs. Then, as soon as they got the e-mail, they would make a phone call to a taxi company and request a taxi to the informed address. Bingo! With that, it all began! The founders validated their primary business hypothesis: many people were willing to call a taxi via website."

MINIMIZE RISKS WITH SEGMENTED PERSONAS

The participants of the Lean Inception already thought about the MVP and its features. They also did the activity on personas and, probably, made considerations about them in order to decide about the MVP.

But, as they fill out the **segmented personas** in the MVP Canvas, they will be demonstrating their decisions straight away. While filling out the MVP Canvas, the question about personas is different from the reflection about personas at the beginning of the Inception. We are no longer talking about the product personas as a whole, we are being more specific.

 Who is this specific MVP for? Can we segment and test this MVP in a smaller group?

By answering these questions, the group must deliberate on the MVP release and how to minimize its risks. For instance, the group may decide that an MVP will be restricted to a smaller group of people and that the same set of features will only be released for a larger group after verifying the expected result.

IMPROVE THE USERS JOURNEYS EXPERIENCE

If the group went through the Lean Inception, the journeys will still be visible, showing the mapped personas, their goals, and features. But even if the group doesn't have the journeys visible, the question must be asked and the information on the improved journeys must be answered on the canvas:

 Which journeys will be complied or improved by this MVP?

The journey maps the experience you provide your users. The answer to this question clearly demonstrates what your MVP is doing for the users.

While filling out the MVP Canvas, the conversations about journeys should be more focused than ones that happened during the activity "Show the journeys" of the Lean Inception. When filling out the MVP canvas, you should consider (and take notes of) only the journey(s) of the segmented people served or improved in the MVP.

If you have difficulty describing at least one journey, reassess—perhaps your MVP does not contemplate anything for anyone (are you releasing less than the minimum viable?). On the other hand, if you add too many journeys to the MVP canvas, re-evaluate it as well—perhaps your MVP is too broad (remember that the "M" of MVP is for minimal, not for maximum). An MVP

Canvas instance must not contemplate all users journeys. These will be contemplated as the product evolves.

REASSESS THE MVP FEATURES

The sequencer demonstrates the feature list for the MVP; that's a great start. Now, you should analyze the already filled out blocks—MVP proposal, segmented personas, and journeys. Review the feature list and ask the following questions:

- » Are they really the minimum?
- » Will they make the product viable?
- » Could we create something even simpler?
- » Did we forget to include something essential to the MVP?

Make any necessary adjustments and changes. At the end, reread the feature block and make sure the following questions have been answered:

 What are we going to build in this MVP? What actions will be simplified or improved in this MVP?

VALIDATE THE BUSINESS HYPOTHESES

User-centered design. That is what we want. In order to create the MVP, we should consider the users and their journeys. We should work on the actions that improve or simplify their lives.

But that is not all. We must describe the hypotheses of the business. We must understand if we are really moving forward, if we are really reaching the desired results or learning.

After defining the MVP features, we must connect them to the expected results and to the business hypotheses. The following model helps with such statement:

> We believe this MVP will achieve _____
> _____(expected result)_____.
>
> We will know that this happened based on _____
> _____(metrics to validate the business hypotheses)_____

The team must fill it out, because, if they don't, they will not know what to expect from the MVP or how to measure it. In both scenarios, the product is drifting, with no direction. Do not create features for a product if you are not able to describe what to expect as a result and how to measure such result.

The above model is an adaptation of Jeff Gothelf's model for hypothesis driven development. This powerful hypotheses-based decision tool is embodied in the MVP Canvas in the "**expected result**" and the "**metrics to validate the business hypotheses**" blocks.

Which learning or result are we searching for in this MVP? How can we measure this? Important note: Do no create features for a product if you can't describe what you expect as a result and how to measure it.

It is important to highlight that learning is also a result. But in order to learn we, at least, must state this: "The expected result is to learn." Then we try to collect data in order to reach the desired learning.

REMEMBER THAT THE "M" OF MVP IS FOR **MINIMAL**, NOT FOR MAXIMUM

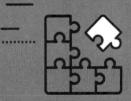

TALK ABOUT COST AND SCHEDULE

Inevitably, right after you answer what the MVP is (and that will be very well represented in the first six blocks of the MVP canvas), you will be asked "When?" and "How much?"

 What is the cost and the schedule for this MVP?

In the MVP Canvas, this question is purposely left to be answered last, as it should only be dealt with after the other blocks are filled out. It is important for everyone to participate in this conversation and to answer this question. Estimating is a sensitive topic; there are lots of techniques to help with this, and many great people to alert you about the problems with estimates.

As Ron Jeffries, one of Extreme Programming forerunners, said, "Estimates are difficult when requirements are vague—and it seems they always are. [...] Even with clear requirements—and they never seem to be—it is still almost impossible to know how long it will take."[12]

Earlier in this book, a sample calculation was demonstrated to aid the understanding of the effort, time, and cost associated with creating the MVP features. That is the one I mostly use when filling out this MVP Canvas block. In my experience, it is better to have the conversation and decide on something than to leave it blank (the blank block might mean different things for different people).

In addition to the cost of creation, what other costs are associated with this MVP? For example: Do we have any marketing campaigns associated with it? Any other expenses? Consider the answers to all questions that come up when detailing the cost of MVP.

12 Available at: <https://ronjeffries.com/xprog/articles/the-noestimates-movement/>. Access in: Aug. 2019.

And often, together with the cost question, the schedule question also comes up. Again, the sample calculation presented earlier helps to understand the period to create the MVP features. Besides these, what else is needed for MVP? Any infrastructure work before you start working on the MVP? Is there any external dependency? Is there a date or time for this to happen? Consider the answers to these questions that come up to create the MVP schedule.

A common consideration for the MVP schedule is about what happens after releasing it. Typically, you are seeking data to validate your business hypotheses. In such case, you should specify (in the schedule) how long after the MVP release date the group should meet and look at the data for further decisions. Eric Ries calls this the "pivot or persevere meeting": **a gathering including the Lean Inception participants and the business leadership to decide to PIVOT[13] or to persevere.**

THE MVP STRATEGY VIA LEAN STARTUP AND DESIGN THIKING

The MVP Canvas is a tool used to validate product ideas. It is a visual board that helps a group of people to align and to define the MVP strategy. The canvas has elements that describe the proposal of MVP, the business hypotheses with their metrics, the personas and their journeys, the features and how much it costs, and how long it takes to create and evaluate them. From Lean Startup, we have the build-measure-learn loop. This loop is represented by the following sections: **features, expected results**, and **metrics for hypotheses validation feature**, which answer the following questions: What are we going to build in this MVP? How will we measure the results of this MVP? What learning or results are we seeking in this MVP?

---

13 Available at: <http://pearllanguage.org/Pivot>. Access in: Aug. 2019.

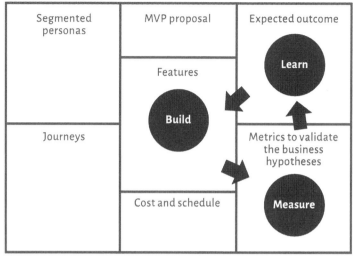

Build in order to learn

MVP Canvas and build-measure-learn loop

The build-measure-learn loop seems to be direct, but it is hard to put it into practice due to the combination of an experimentation approach (build to learn) with a design mindset (learn to build). In order to help understand and build the MVP, we complement this loop with another one: user-journey-action, which brings us to a Design Thinking approach, focusing on learning about personas and their journeys.

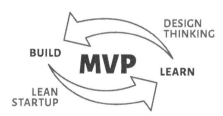

Build in order to learn or learn in order to build

Whom is this MVP for? Which journey will be improved in this MVP? Which action will be simplified or improved by this MVP? The answer to these three questions complete the user-journey-action loop.

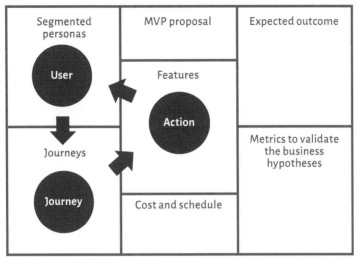

MVP Canvas and user-journey-action loop

While filling out the MVP Canvas, we put the two loops side by side—the build-measure-learn loop from Lean Startup and the user-journey-action loop from Design thinking.

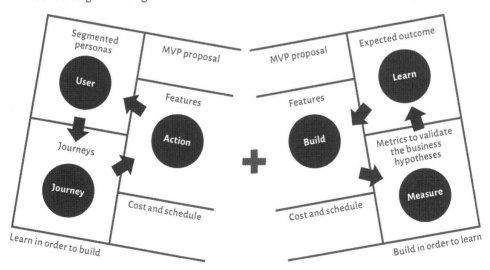

MVP Canvas = learn in order to build + build in order to learn

The loops overlap in the feature section: Which features are going to be built for this MVP? Note that this question can be put in two different ways: 1- What are we going to **build** in this MVP? and 2- Which **actions** are going to be simplified or improved by this MVP?

Build, from Lean Startup, or **action**, from Design Thinking. Both refer to the MVP features available for their users. For such reason, the feature section is right in the center of the canvas, representing its central point.

> *"Great things are not done by impulse, but by a series of small things brought together."*

Vincent Van Gogh

Thank you for following me during the journey of Lean Inception. I hope this makes so much difference in your business and that your MVP will be very successful.

APPENDIX

LEAN INCEPTION EXAMPLE

"I would like to see a complete example of a Lean Inception." That is a recurring request from the readers. I imagine that reading can be made easier for those who have already taken part in a workshop or in a Lean Inception. Although the book explains the recipe items and the step-by-step for each activity, I understand it is still worth demonstrating a complete example. That is what I am going to share in this chapter.

For confidentiality reasons regarding the companies that hired me to facilitate these Lean Inceptions, I won't be able to share the results of the activities for their products. Many of them started as lean products with their incremental MVPs, and today they are unique products in their fields. For such reason, I have selected a real, very well-illustrated example that can be shared. This lean product was designed during a Lean Inception workshop that took place as a tutorial during a large conference. Because there were more than 20 participants attending the workshop, the product was designed and shared with everyone.

As the workshop would take eight hours, the typical weekly schedule of a Lean Inception was compressed in order to fit in a few hours. The burn-up agenda was essential to keep everyone aligned on how fast the rhythm we had to follow for that event would be.

I reiterate that the following content and photos are from an example made in one day, therefore, it is probably short on the amount of generated artifacts: personas, journeys, and features. The goal was to reach the minimum necessary for each activity, in order to demonstrate the activities technique and simulate the Lean Inception collaborative environment.

KICK-OFF

The day started with an icebreaker. I used Zip Zap Zoom. That lasted less than ten minutes and was very useful to get everyone to share their names. We started the day with lots of energy and having a good laugh.

Then I made a brief presentation about Lean Inception (the same presentation I use for the Lean Inception workshop kick-offs in companies). This helps to align the concept of MVP and to explain the sequence of activities that will be performed.

Instead of the typical kick-off, usually made by stakeholders talking about the product or the idea to be conceived during a Lean Inception, the workshop kick-off had a different style. I asked the participants who had an idea of a product and wanted to explore it as an example for the workshop throughout the day. Three participants presented three different product ideas. Then, everyone voted for the one that they wanted to use in the workshop.

WRITE THE PRODUCT VISION DOWN

The most voted product was a soccer app for friends. The users would be people who enjoy playing soccer with their friends from work, from the gym, or some group of people scheduling a game.

> For soccer players
>
> who have a hard time finding soccer matches.
>
> The Easy-bola
>
> is a mobile app
>
> that makes it easy to find matches.
>
> Instead of word of mouth
>
> our product maximizes the chances of finding a pick-up soccer game

This is the result of the product vision for the app idea to organize soccer players and soccer matches. The following activities in this chapter are about Easy-bola. Such activities help to understand the lean product, the MVPs built for creating and validating this mobile app.

THE PRODUCT IS – IS NOT – DOES – DOES NOT DO

The activity Is – Is Not – Does – Does Not Do helps define Easy-bola. That helped to clarify the product idea, focusing on MVP and eliminating an initial excess of features. At this point, important conversations came up, such as:

» This app will be free of charge.

» There is not going to be a site or online version.

» Geolocation is very interesting.

» This app does not create teams, manage payments or organize championships.

Check out the transcriptions of the Post-Its wrote during the activity.

- » **What the product is:** App, mobile app, multi-platform, facilitator for organizing pick up soccer matches, free.
- » **What the product is not:** Facebook, Twitter, WhatsApp, a site, a chat, a messenger (chat).
- » **What the product does:** Schedule matches (agenda), schedule fields, list matches, locate nearby pick-up soccer matches, geolocation, alert on events, notify users, rating users, evaluate reputation.
- » **What the product does not do:** Organize matches, define teams by request, organize matches and teams, assemble teams, manage payments, provide online payment of the match, schedule private matches, organize championships, create championships.

UNDERSTANDING GOALS

After the previous activities, we executed the activity that would explain the goals of the product. At this point, we asked all participants to share their understanding on the three main goals of the product. Each one wrote three Post-Its. After collecting and organizing them in affinity groups, three main product goals were identified:

- » Finding matches
- » Promoting matches
- » Matches options

DESCRIBE THE PERSONAS

After a good understanding of the product, it was time to change the focus and look for a good understanding regarding personas, the users of the product. In order to do that, we used the quadrant template to identify the types of personas. With such template, we created nicknames for each type, describe their profiles, their behavioral characteristics, and their particular needs. Even with the short time, all participants took part in groups that created personas while having fun with their descriptions, nicknames, and drawings.

In order to create personas, the twenty participants were divided into three smaller groups. Each group created two or three personas and presented them to all workshop participants. Next, the duplicate (or very similar) personas were discarded, and all participants voted on the top four personas for the product.

Check out the text transcription of the most voted persona: the soccer dude.

- » **Nickname:** Soccer dude.
- » **Profile:** 28 years-old, married, frustrated player, works for a bank, undergraduate degree.
- » **Behavior:** Complainer, competitive, active, picky with the field, spends hours on social networks.
- » **Needs:** To play every week with anyone and anywhere, but looks for high-performance matches, plays at night on weekends.

FEATURES BRAINSTORMING

After we had developed the product, goals, and personas, it was time to think and let the new features (foreseen functionalities for the lean product). For this, we used the discovering features activity.

Features have already appeared several times in previous conversations. Now it was really the time to brainstorm and write them.

Note that the goals are on the canvas as column titles, while the personas are acting as row titles. This builds the canvas so that the features are discovered. Thus, the facilitator is able to promote a brainstorming on the features.

What must there be in the product to fulfill this persona's needs? Which features should we build in order to achieve this goal? With these questions in mind, the discussion is guided so that we discover which features are necessary to reach goals and personas. They are written in Post-Its and placed on the canvas. The question is repeated for each goal-persona combination, thus prioritizing the main goals and main personas.

Check out the transcription of the features Post-Its for the Easy-bola Lean Inception.

- » Check for matches with geolocation
- » Check for matches without geolocation
- » Field ranking
- » Rank a player
- » Match details (place, time, and date)
- » Players ranking (visualization)
- » Financial details of the match
- » Player registry
- » Match registry
- » Invitations to the match for friends
- » Detailed filter
- » Alert mode
- » RSVP
- » Alert for confirmed match
- » Alert for canceled match

» Attendance canceling

» Match canceling

TECHNICAL, UX, AND BUSINESS REVIEW

The features were discovered, but they were accepted with no questions asked, without spending much time understanding their details, making notes or talking about uncertainties, efforts, and value for the business and for the users.

However, these conversations and more detailed information are very useful for a better understanding and planning on creating lean products. The technical and business understanding and the effort and business value activities and graphics look for such information in a fast and efficient way.

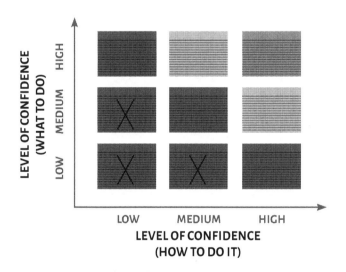

Each feature was plotted on the graph and on the table, and received markings of uncertainty level, effort, and business value. In the graph the feature received a color. On the table, the feature received markings of value and effort. In addition, all extra information about the feature was described in Post-Its and put behind the feature card. These are two examples: 1- use lib from Google to geolocation, and 2- assume that it will only work in the most modern mobile devices.

Check the table below with the result of this activity, now with the features and their markings in the canvas with goals, personas, and features. In this table, the color on the feature card represents the level of uncertainty of the feature: red for a high uncertainty level, yellow for medium, and green for low. Meanwhile, the markings of UX value, business value, and effort vary in a scale of one, two or three, comparatively; that is, one, two or three hearts to small, medium, and high UX value, respectively; $, $$, $$$ to high, very high, and skyrocketing business value, respectively; and E, EE, EEE for low, medium, and high effort, respectively. The colors and markings on the features helped the participants in the subsequent activities of prioritizing, estimating, and planning MVPs.

FEATURE	UNCERTAINTY	EFFORT	UX VALUE	BUSINESS VALUE
CHECK FOR MATCHES WITH GEOLOCATION	YELLOW	EE	♡♡♡	$$$
CHECK FOR MATCHES WITHOUT GEOLOCATION	RED	E	♡♡	$$
FIELD RANKING	RED	E	♡♡♡	$
RANK A PLAYER	GREEN	EE	♡♡	$
MATCH DETAILS (PLACE, TIME AND DAY)	RED	E	♡♡♡	$$

PLAYER RANKING (VISUALIZATION)	YELLOW	EE	♡♡	$
FINANCIAL DETAILS OF THE MATCH	RED	E	♡	$$
PLAYER REGISTER	RED	E	♡	$
MATCH REGISTER	RED	E	♡♡♡	$$$
INVITE FRIEND FOR A MATCH	YELLOW	EE	♡♡♡	$$
DETAILED FEATURE	RED	EE	♡	$$
ALERT MODE	GREEN	EEE	♡♡	$
RSVP	RED	E	♡♡	$$$
ALERT FOR CONFIRMED MATCH	RED	EE	♡♡	$$$
ALERT FOR CANCELED MATCH	RED	EE	♡	$$$
PARTICIPATION CANCELING	RED	E	♡♡	$$$
MATCH CANCELING	RED	EE	♡♡	$$$

SHOW THE USERS' JOURNEYS

At this point, we went back to the personas perspective, now focusing on their journeys, the step-by-step tasks to reach a goal. The participants were divided into groups again. Each group selected a persona and identified the main scenarios for such persona to reach the main goals. The step-by-step of each one was described in Post-Its on a flipchart.

The following questions helped the beginning of journey description:

» What goal does this persona want to reach?

» How does this persona start the day?

» What does this persona do after that in order to reach the goal?

Next, there are two examples of journeys:

SOCCER DUDE CREATES A MATCH

» Wakes up early for work

» Eats a lot at breakfast

» Arrives for work at 9:00 a.m.

» During a meeting, decides to engage in a physical activity

» At a lunch, talks a friend from the office into playing soccer after work

» Calls and books a court

» Opens Easy-bola

» Sets the match for 8:00 p.m. on that same day

» Fills out the information about the court

» Sends invitation to friends

WORK BUDDY: ACCEPTS INVITE FOR A MATCH

» Wakes up late for work

» Eats a cereal bar in the subway

» Arrives for work at 9:30 a.m.

» Goes to the gym at lunchtime

» During a meeting, gets an alert from Easy-bola

» Checks match information

» Checks the field ranking

» RSVPs to match

» Leaves meeting for another meeting

» At 5:14 p.m. gets match confirmation

DISPLAY FEATURES IN JOURNEYS

Note that some of the steps of the journeys described here represent different contact points with the product, characterizing the user interaction with it. This was the time to check every analysis made up to now, comparing these contact points to the product to the features and its information.

Check the example of the previous journey, now with features in some steps.

WORK BUDDY: ACCEPTING INVITES FOR A MATCH

STEP	FEATURE
WAKES UP LATE FOR WORK	-
EATS A CEREAL BAR IN THE SUBWAY	-
ARRIVES FOR WORK AT 9:30 A.M.	-
GOES TO GYM AT LUNCHTIME	-
DURING A MEETING, GETS AN ALERT FROM EASY-BOLA	ALERT MODE
CHECKS MATCH INFORMATION	MATCH DETAILS (PLACE, TIME AND DAY)
CHECKS THE FIELD RANKING	FIELD RANKING
RSVPs TO MATCH	RSVP
LEAVES MEETING TO ANOTHER MEETING	-
AT 5:14 P.M. GETS MATCH CONFIRMATION	ALERT FOR CONFIRMED MATCH

SEQUENCE THE FEATURES

Now it was time to build the features sequencer. This is the moment when every analysis up to this point (products, personas, features and journeys) is put to the test in a canvas containing simple and essential rules to organize and visualize the features and their relation to MVPs.

As a facilitator, I described the rules of the features sequencer and left the participants free to organize the features on the sequencer. The following image shows every participant involved searching for features in the journeys and putting them on the sequencer.

While participants choose and order the features on the features sequencer, I wrote on a few Post-Its: MVP1, MVP2, MVP3, and so on. I asked them to verify when a feature composition reached a simple version of the product that could be made available. If so, a Post-It was placed on the right side of the flipchart, identifying the features of an MVP.

Below, the transcription of the features sequencer of Easy-bola shown in the illustration, with its identified MVPs and respective features.

FEATURE	WAVE	MVP
REGISTER MATCH	1	1
REGISTER PLAYER	1	1
SEARCH FOR MATCHES WITHOUT GEOLOCATION	1	1
CONFIRM PRESENCE	2	2
DETAILING MATCH (PLACE, HOUR AND DATE)	2	2
CANCEL PRESENCE	2	2
CANCEL MATCH	3	3
NOTIFICATION MODULE	3	3
NOTIFICATION FOR CONFIRMED MATCH	4	3
NOTIFICATION FOR CANCELED MATCH	4	3
FINANCIAL DETAILS OF MATCH	4	4
INVITE FRIEND TO MATCH	5	4
RANKING OF PLAYERS (VISUALIZATION)	5	4

BUILD THE MVP CANVAS

After deciding on MVPs in the features sequencer, it was time to detail the first MVP. For this we use the MVP canvas. Below is the image with the result of MVP Canvas for MVP1.

Next, the transcription of the MVP Canvas for EasyBola MVP1 presented in the image, with its translated notes for each of the seven canvas blocks.

MVP PROPOSAL

» Validate if the residents of the Pinheiros neighborhood will use the app to schedule matches.

SEGMENTED PERSONAS

» Soccer dude

» Lonely player

» Small neighborhood in São Paulo

JOURNEYS

» Soccer dude registers a game

» Player registers and searches for a game

FEATURES

» Player registry, only for Android devices

» Soccer match registry, only for Android devices

» Enquiry of soccer match without geolocation, only for Android devices

EXPECTED RESULTS

» 200 users within one month

» 50 matches in the first month

» 300 downloads within one month

METRICS TO VALIDATE BUSINESS HYPOTHESES

» Number of users registered in the database

» Number of matches registered in the database

» Number of app downloads in the play store

COSTS & SCHEDULE

» Two weeks to create the app, two developers

» $ 3,000.00 in online marketing and flyers (in neighborhood blocks)

GLOSSARY

A A short list of terms is used in this book. Each of the concepts is explored in detail in the main chapters. However, I believe it is necessary to have a definition, even at a high level, for these terms, from the beginning. This list of terms must be visible during the Inception Workshop. I suggest printing this glossary and placing it on the wall of the war room.

PERSONA A persona represents a user of the product, describing not only his or her role, but also his or her specific needs. This creates a realistic representation of users, helping the team to describe features from the point of view of those who will interact with the final product.

FEATURE Feature is the description of an action or interaction of a user with the product. For example: print invoice, see detailed statement, and invite Facebook friends.

FEATURE TECHNICAL CONFIDENCE The understanding of the feature considering the technical challenges, the dependencies, and the infrastructure requirements. Have you done this before? Do you know **how** to do it? A strong yes indicates a high level of confidence.

FEATURE UX AND BUSINESS CONFIDENCE The understanding of the feature regarding what to build, both from the business point of view and from the usability point of view. Do you know WHAT the business and/or user wants from this feature? A strong yes indicates a high level of certainty.

FEATURE EFFORT The level of the work that needs to be done in a feature. The understanding of the team according the difficulty and the work that is going to be necessary to complete such feature.

FEATURE BUSINESS VALUE The business value, the ROI (return on investment) of the feature, a measurement according to the business on how much this feature is worth. What is the return or savings that a feature will bring?

FEATURE UX VALUE The User eXperience value, the expected value of the feature for the users, a measurement by the users on how much they want this feature. What is the perceived value (in hearts) a feature will bring to the users?

USER JOURNEY The user journey describes the path a user takes through a sequence of steps offered to reach a goal. Some of these steps represent different points of contact with the product, featuring the interaction of the user with it.

MVP The Minimum Viable Product (MVP) is the simplest version of a product that may be available for business. The MVP defines which are the essential features for the minimal functional product that may add value to the business (minimal product) and that can be used and validated by the final user (viable product).

ICEBREAKERS

ICEBREAKERS

Icebreakers are activities to warm up the team and promote group interaction. It is a good starter for any team meeting. It is extra valuable for early stages of team building and intensive workshops such as Lean Inceptions. An activity called Punctual Paulo has already been demonstrated before.

This appendix presents even more icebreaker ideas for your Lean Inception. Such activities have been cordially shared from the website and book *Fun Retrospectives*.

For more activities check out: www.funretrospectives.com/category/energizer.

GEOGRAPHIC LOCATION

This activity is a good icebreaker and also helps team members to learn a little bit about each other.

ACTIVITY STEP BY STEP

1. Explain to the participants that each one will be a geographic location (for example: their country, city or neighborhood).
2. Show where the north and the south are in the room.
3. Ask each participant to move to where he thinks he belongs in order to create a map as close to scale as possible.

4. After everyone moves to their spot, ask one volunteer to draw a map representing the room.

VISUAL PHONE

Visual phone is a great energizer to get everyone engaged while fostering a conversation about communication and its interpretations.

ACTIVITY STEP BY STEP

1. Divide the large group into sets of three people (one or two groups can have four people).

2. Place three Post-Its and a pen in front of each person.

3. Ask everyone to write a sentence (on the Post-It), then place a blank Post-It on top of it (at this point, only the author of the sentence knows what it is).

4. Everyone passes the Post-It clockwise.

5. Each person reads the sentence from the Post-It in front of him/her, and then creates a representative drawing for the sentence (on the blank Post-It).

6. Everyone passes the Post-Its clockwise.

7. On a new Post-It, each person writes a sentence for the drawing in front of him/her, and places it on top of the Post-It set (now the set has three Post-Its: the original sentence, the drawing, and the new sentence).

8. Everyone passes the Post-It set clockwise (for the groups of three people, the set should end up in front of the original sentence writer).

9. Open the Post-It set so everyone can see the sentences and their respective drawings.

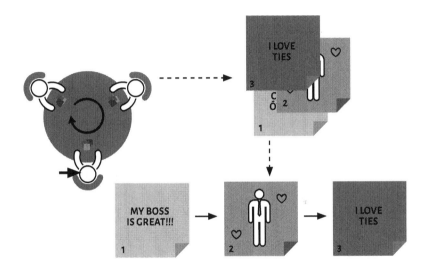

Typically, the participants will laugh and have a great time comparing drawings and sentences.

This is a great energizer with a subtle message about communication (both visual and written), context, and interpretations. This is an adaptation from an activity we learned in a UX (User eXperience) workshop presented by my dear UX friends Natalia Arsand, Juliana Dorneles, and Gabriel Albo. They learned it from the Human Centered Design workshop by IDEO.

ONE TWO PING FOUR PONG

This is a short activity to start up a meeting in a good mood and get participants engaged.

ACTIVITY STEP BY STEP

1. Ask the participants to form a circle.

2. The participants must decide which direction to follow (clockwise or counterclockwise).

3. Someone starts by saying any positive number that is not a multiple of 3 or 5.

4. The next person, following the direction, mentally increments the number by one. So:

   ▸ If the number is not a multiple of 3 or 5: Says the number

   ▸ If the number is a multiple of 3: Says ping and claps

   ▸ If the number is a multiple of 5: Says pong and jumps

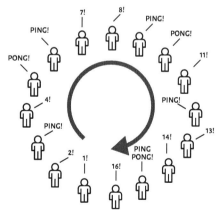

For large groups, it is recommended to remove a person from the circle for making a mistake or erroneously accusing someone. Soon, everyone will be laughing and cheering for the remaining ones.

FORMING TRIANGLES

This activity is a great energizer with a valuable message, and is very useful in starting a conversation about self-organizing teams.

ACTIVITY STEP BY STEP

This activity is divided in two parts.

FIRST PART:

1. Ask the members of the group to walk individually in a random direction.
2. After some time, say the magic word "triangle." Each group member will have to find two other people and form an equilateral triangle (each person is a triangle vertex and should point each arm towards the other two people representing the other triangle vertices; each person is a triangle vertex in one triangle only).
3. Check how long it took for the group to form the triangles.

SECOND PART:

1. Select one person to be the foreman of the group triangle.
2. Ask the members of the group to walk in a random direction.

3. After some time, say the magic word, "triangle". The foreman has to form equilateral triangles with all group members (including him/herself in one of the triangles).

4. Check how long it took for the group to form the triangles.

The first part shows a self-organizing group; the second part shows a group guided by one organizer (the foreman).

Typically, the self-organizing triangle formation runs faster than its counterpart, and the team feels more engaged in the activity.

This activity was borrowed from Heitor Roriz, a friend and scrum coach and trainer. Kudos to him for applying a fun activity to fostering the conversation about an essential concept of successful agile teams: self-organization.

ZIP ZAP ZOOM

This is a good meeting starter, especially for new teams. It brings energy to the room and the activity dynamics helps the participants to remember each other's names.

ACTIVITY STEP BY STEP

1. Ask the team to form a circle, and each participant to point their index fingers.

2. Explain the verbal commands.

3. Ask a participant to make the first movement, saying one of the verbal commands and choosing the initial direction (clockwise or counterclockwise).

THE VERBAL COMMANDS

Each participant should, at his/her turn, make a verbal command, pointing to a receiver. The verbal command should be one of the following:

- **Zip:** Point to the person exactly at your side, keeping the previous direction.
- **Zap:** Point to the person exactly at your side, changing the previous direction.
- **Zoom:** Point to anyone in the circle, saying his/her name. The receiver should decide the direction for the next movement during his/her turn.

When a participant executes an incorrect command (either a command that doesn't exist or pointing to the wrong direction in a zip/zap command), he/she should be removed from the circle.

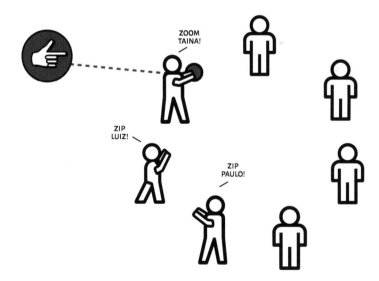

This activity is not only a good energizer but also pushes the participants to focus and helps them remember each other's names.

UNTANGLE YOURSELVES

Untangle yourselves is a great energizer to get people moving. It has a very interesting message on finding your way out of a tangled situation.

ACTIVITY STEP BY STEP

1. Ask the group to form a circle.

2. Ask everyone put their hands up.

3. Give the tangling instructions.

   - With your right hand, grab someone's left hand.
   - With your left hand, grab someone's right hand.
   - You cannot grab the hands of the people next to you.

4. Ask the group to untangle itself without letting go of the hands, and trying to form a circle.

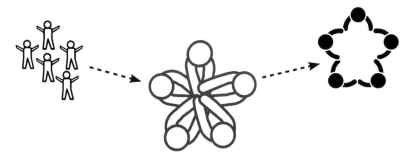

The group will skip hands, switch around and find a way out, either forming one or more circles. Sometimes, it is not possible to untangle. In such scenario, ask the group to select one person to be removed. Hands that become free should reconnect to the person remaining on the tangled group.

Group size: larger than six people, up to any number. For very large groups, break into smaller groups of approximately twelve people.

BALLOON BATTLE

The Balloon Battle is a great energizer to get everyone moving while creating a situation to introduce some concepts like team strategy, team work, collaboration, partnership, and win-win situations.

ACTIVITY STEP BY STEP

1. Instruct everyone to tie a balloon to his/her left foot (you will need balloons and strings for all participants).

2. Divide the group into several smaller groups.

3. Instruct everyone about the team's mission and the game duration: "All teams have the same goal: to protect the team balloons. The game goes on for three minutes. At the end we will count and announce the team with the highest number of full balloons."

4. Say GO! and count down three minutes.

Typically, the participants will have lots of fun. Many people might run around and attack other people's balloons. At the end of the game you can have conversations about teamwork, team strategy, perception of responsibility, and our favorite: the competitive human nature, which at times works against a win-win situation. For instance, if no one moves and attacks other people's balloons, every team accomplishes the goal of protecting the team's balloons, and every team ends up with the highest number of full balloons. Interestingly enough, we have never seen or heard of this outcome.

COMPLEX PIECES

Complex Pieces is a great energizer to get people moving around while fostering a conversation about complex systems and interconnected pieces.

ACTIVITY STEP BY STEP

1. Everybody stands up and walks around.
2. Each person thinks about two other people.
3. Without giving names, each person should stay equally distant from the two people they thought about. It should take one minute for people to move around.
4. After people stop moving, ask the tallest person in the group to move to a corner of the room.
5. Ask everyone to find their equal distances again.

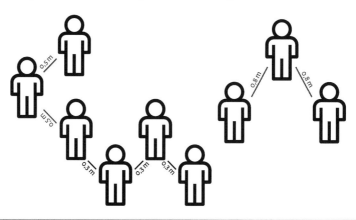

We have learned this activity from Bethlem Migot. She used it as an energizer during an analysis workshop. It got everyone energized before she had a quick conversation about complex systems, changes, and interconnected requirements. This activity works best for a group of ten to thirty people.

COLLABORATIVE FACE DRAWING

The collaborative face drawing is a fun interactive activity that helps with name memorization.

ACTIVITY STEP BY STEP

1. Give each participant one US Letter or A4 paper and a pen.
2. Instruct the participants to write their name on the bottom of the paper.
3. Ask everyone to walk randomly around the room until you say "stop."
4. Each person should pair up with someone nearby.
5. Instruct the pair to exchange papers.
6. Everyone should draw the other person's eyes.
7. Instruct the pairs to exchange papers again (now each person should have the paper with their name again).
8. Repeat steps 3 to 7 for all face parts (eyes, nose, ears, chin, hair, facial hair, and accessories).

BACK TO BACK

Back to Back is a fun energetic activity with a strong and simple message about collaborative work.

ACTIVITY STEP BY STEP

1. Instruct the participants to find a pair of similar height and weight.
2. Ask everyone to sit on the floor, back to back with their pair.
3. Ask the pairs to hold each other's arms while keeping their backs together.
4. Tell everyone their goal is to stand up, while keeping arms and backs together.

This activity is really fun. People will laugh. Typically, a few pairs will be able to stand up faster, while others will have a hard time. Consider not running this activity if you feel some participant is not capable of standing up will feel bad by sitting on the floor.

FIND YOUR PAIR

Find Your Pair is a really funny energizer to get everyone moving and laughing.

ACTIVITY STEP BY STEP

1. Count the number of participants (an even number is required, so decide whether or not to include yourself).

2. Divide the number of participants by two to decide how many animals will be used (let's say there are twenty participants, so there will be ten different animals).

3. Write each animal's name on two Post-Its.

4. Hand the Post-Its to the participants and tell them not to show them to anyone.

5. Ask everyone to move around in the room.

6. Instruct everyone to cover their eyes with their hands, make the animal noise and try to find their pair.

I have learned this activity from Bethlem Migot. I confess it took me a while to get used to it. But I decided to give it a try after watching it being used so many times, and people always enjoyed it. I would only recommend being cautious about cultural differences and making sure the participants are already used to energizers.

REFERENCES

AGUIAR, Fábio; CAROLI, Paulo. *Product Backlog Building*: Construção de um Product Backlog efetivo. LeanPub, 2018.

BECK, Kent. *Extreme Programming Explained: Embrace Change*. Addison Wesley Professional, 1999.

BLANK, Steve G. *The Four Steps to the Epiphany*: Successful Strategies for Products that Win. 5th ed. K&S Ranch, 2013.

Burn-up agenda. Available on: <www.caroli.org/en/burn-up-agenda/>. Access in: July 2019.

CAROLI, Paulo; CAETANO, Tain. *Fun Retrospectives*: Activities and Ideas for Making Agile Retrospectives More Engaging. LeanPub, 2014.

CAROLI, Paulo. *Direto ao Ponto*: Criando Produtos de Forma Enxuta. Casa do Código, 2014.

CAROLI, PAULO. *Lean Inception*. Available on: <martinfowler.com/articles/lean-inception>. Access in: July 2019.

CAROLI, Paulo. *MVPs no Mundo Real: O Caso do EasyTaxi* (2015). Available on: <www.infoq.com/br/articles/mvp-easy-taxi>. Access in: July 2019.

CAROLI, PAULO. *The MVP Canvas*. Available on: <www.caroli.org/en/the-mvp-canvas/>. Access in: July 2019.

COHN, Mike. *User Stories Applied*: For Agile Software Development. Addison-Wesley Professional, 2004.

COOPER, A.; REIMANN, R.; CRONIN, D.; NOESSEL, C. *About Face*: The Essentials of Interaction Design. 4th ed. Wiley, 2014.

GOTHELF, Jeff; SEIDEN, Josh. *Lean UX*: Applying Lean Principles to Improve User Experience. O'Reilly Media, 2013.

GRANDONI, Dino. *How Long People Waited to Be First in Line to Buy Apple Products* (2011). Available on: <https://www.theatlantic.com/technology/archive/2011/

10/how-long-people-waited-be-first-line-buy-apple-products/337087/>. Access in: July 2019.

GOMES, Tallis. *Nada easy*: O passo a passo de como combinei gestão, inovação e criatividade para levar minha empresa a 35 países em quatro anos. Editora Gente, 2017.

HUMBLE, Jez; FARLEY, David. *Continuous Delivery*: Reliable Software Releases through Build, Test and Deployment Automation. Addison-Wesley Professional, 2010.

JEFFRIES, Ron. *The Noestimates Movement* (2013). Available on: <ronjeffries.com/xprog/articles/the-noestimates-movement>. Access in: July 2019.

LOWDERMILK, Travis. *User-centered Design*: A Developer's Guide to Building Userfriendly Applications. O'Reilly Media, 2013.

MCCLURE, Dave. *Métricas de Pirata – AARRR*. Available on: <pt.wikipedia.org/wiki/AARRR>. Access in: July 2019.

OHNO, Taiichi. *Toyota Production System*. Productivity Press, 1988.

OSTERWALDER, A.; PIGNEUR, Y. *Business Model Generation*: A Handbook for Visionaries, Game Changers and Challengers. OSF, 2009.

PATTON, Jeff. *User Story Mapping*: Discover the Whole Story, Build the Right Product. O'Reilly Media, 2014.

Pragmatic Personas. Available on: <www.stickyminds.com/article/pragmatic-personas>. Access in: jul. 2019.

Principles Behind the Agile Manifesto (2001). Available on: <www.agilemanifesto.org/principles.html>. Access in: July 2019.

RASMUSSON, Jonathan. *The Agile Samurai*: How Agile Masters Deliver Great Software. Pragmatic Bookshelf, 2010.

RIES, Eric. *The Lean Startup*: How Today's Entrepreneurs Use Continuous Innovation to Create Radically Successful Businesses. Crown Publishing, 2011.

RIES, Eric. *The Startup Way*: How Modern Companies Use Entrepreneurial Management to Transform Culture and Drive Long-Term Growth. Redfern: Currency, 2017.

SABBAGH, Rafael. *Scrum*: Gestão Ágil para Projetos de Sucesso. Casa do Código, 2013.

SCHWABER, Ken; BEEDLE, Mike. *Agile Software Development with Scrum*. Pearson, 2001.

SUTHERLAND, Jeff. *Scrum*: The Art of Doing Twice the Work in Half the Time. Crown Business, 2014.

TAYLOR, Jeffrey L. *Hypothesis-Driven Development*, Article on Dr. Dobb's (2011), Available on: <www.drdobbs.com/architecture-and-design/hypothesis-driven-development/229000656>. Access in: July 2019.

WILLIAN, S. Junk. *The Dynamic Balance Between Cost, Schedule, Features and Quality in Software Development Projects*. Computer Science Department, University of Idaho, SEPM-001, 2000.

WOMACK, James P.; JONES, Daniel T.; ROOS, Daniel. *The Machine that Changed the World*: The Story of Lean Production – Toyota's Secret Weapon in the Global Car Wars that Is Now Revolutionizing World Ind. Free Press; Reprint, 2007.

WOMACK, James P.; JONES, Daniel T. *Lean Thinking*: Banish Waste and Create Wealth in Your Corporation – revised and updated. 2nd ed. Free Press, 2003.

BE A
LEAN INCEPTION
FACILITATOR

At first, I thought that writing the step by step Lean Inception activities in the book would be enough. Over time, however, I realized that the connection between Lean Inception facilitators and the exchange of experience between them is very rich, and this cannot happen with the book alone.

In addition, the demand for Lean Inception facilitators was increasing a lot: companies approached me asking for recommendations for facilitators, and people would ask me for training. So, I got together with other people with a lot of experience in Lean Inception and we started organizing communities and training to share this practice. The trainings started in Brazil on December of 2017 and have been expanding ever since.

Check out the Lean Inception communities at:
www.caroli.org/en/lean-inception-community.
Check out the Lean Inception training at:
www.caroli.org/en/training/lean-inception.

ABOUT EDITORA CAROLI

For readers and authors who seek and share knowledge quickly, Editora Caroli is a small publisher—all books are written, read, edited and/or revised by Paulo Caroli, who assists in the production, dissemination and distribution of books and e-books. Unlike traditional publishing houses, Editora Caroli gives access to knowledge in its essence, offering new content via free e-books, as well as supporting events and educational entities, presenting them with free books and e-books.

At **www.caroli.org** you will find this and other quality content. Enjoy our free materials!

WIP (WRITING IN PROGRESS)

Editora Caroli presents a new work proposal, bringing authors closer to their readers from the beginning of content production. Why wait for the author to finish writing to find out if the content is any good? In today's world this no longer makes sense. For this reason, Editora Caroli promotes sharing (for free whenever possible) of WIP through e-book formats (.pdf, .mobi and .epub). This way, readers have quick access to new ideas and can be part of the development of the work. For the authors, it is an effective form of feedback and motivation for content creation.

PAULO CAROLI is passionate about innovation, entrepreneurship, and digital products. He is a software engineer, author, speaker, and successful facilitator.

Principal consultant at ThoughtWorks and cofounder of AgileBrazil, Paulo Caroli has over twenty years of experience in software development, working in various corporations in Brazil, India, USA, Latin America and Europe. In 2000, he discovered Extreme Programming and, since then, has focused his expertise in processes and practices of Agile & Lean. He joined ThoughtWorks in 2006 and has held the positions of Agile Coach, Trainer and Delivery Manager. Caroli has a Bachelor degree of Computer Science and a MS in Software Engineering, both from PUC-Rio.

Follow Paulo Caroli on his website and on social media:

www.caroli.org

in paulocaroli
🐦 paulocaroli
f Paulo.Caroli

Printed in Great Britain
by Amazon

49442105R00095